Devaki Jain graduated in economics and philosophy from St Anne's College, Oxford. She is now an Honorary Fellow of the college. From 1963-69, she was a lecturer in economics at Miranda House, Delhi University. She moved on from teaching to fulltime research and publication as the director of the Institute of Social Studies Trust. Over the course of her career, Devaki Jain founded a wide range of institutions such as the Development Alternatives for Women for a New Era (DAWN), a Third World network of women social scientists. She has been a member of several policy making bodies in India and abroad, including the State Planning Board of Karnataka; the Advisory Committee for UNDP Human Development Report on Poverty (1997); and the Eminent Persons Group associated with the Graca Machel Committee (UN) on the impact on children of armed conflict. She is a recipient of the Padma Bhushan (2006) and an honorary doctorate from the University of Westville, Durban, South Africa.

Praise for *The Brass Notebook: A Memoir*

'A riveting account of the lifestory of a courageous woman who has all her life challenged what convention expects of her.' —Desmond Tutu

'A remarkable memoir...I met [Devaki Jain] three decades ago and have remained in awe of her: pioneering feminist, economist and Gandhian and social activist.' —Shashi Tharoor

'...a deliciously crafted page-turner that brings forth stories and insights from a lifetime of adventure.' —Chintan Girish Mody, *Business Standard*

'...this thoroughly enjoyable book is a must-read for women to know how to survive and succeed in a patriarchal society [and] for men to know that women are not the weaker sex but just unaware of their inherent strength.' —Renu Sud Sinha in *The Tribune*

'What makes the book enthralling are the fascinating insights into...the personal challenges and emotions that defined various periods of [Jain's] life...she is unflinchingly honest in ways that must have taken both great soul-searching and a level of fearlessness that transcends what people may think.' —Jayati Ghosh in *The Telegraph*

'*The Brass Notebook* is a portrait of a past that feels golden, filled with idealism, grit and hope.' —Deepanjali Pal, *Hindustan Times*

The Brass Notebook

A Memoir

Devaki Jain

SPEAKING TIGER

SPEAKING TIGER BOOKS LLP
125A, Ground Floor, Shahpur Jat, near Asiad Village,
New Delhi 110049

First published in hardback by Speaking Tiger books 2020
First published in paperback by Speaking Tiger Books 2023

ISBN: 978-93-5447-663-1
eISBN: 978-93-89958-68-3

10 9 8 7 6 5 4 3 2 1

Typeset in Sabon LT Std by SÜRYA, New Delhi
Printed at Chaman Enterprises, New Delhi

To Laam, Lammu—otherwise known as Lakshmi Jain
For leading me to utmost happiness
and
Gopal, Smriti and Vasu for keeping me there!

Contents

Foreword

This is a wonderful memoir of someone who has an extraordinary recollection of interesting things happening around her and who writes about them beautifully.

I have had the privilege of knowing Devaki for well over sixty years. When I first met her, I was struck not only by her joyful presence, but also by her remarkable ability to be easily amused.

Devaki was a brilliant student—educated at Mysore University and at Oxford (where she was elected an Honorary Fellow of St Anne's College)—but her fame far exceeded her formal training. She has been widely known for her unusual insights on the place of women in society, particularly on the reach of inequalities based on gender.

Apart from its originality, the memoir is enriched by the fact that throughout her life, Devaki has been close to people of great interest. Her father knew Mahatma Gandhi who told him on the day before his assassination about his premonition about it. Devaki herself walked with Vinoba Bhave and worked with Jayaprakash Narayan.

As a young woman studying in Oxford, she came to know closely the leading academics there—from Iris Murdoch to Jennifer Hart, among many others. She became a good friend of such remarkable personalities as Gloria Steinem, with whom she worked on feminist ideas, and Julius Nyerere, who persuaded her to join him in the famous South Commission, to build a less unjust world. She has worked closely with many political leaders in South Africa, including Nelson Mandela, and Desmond Tutu, and with pioneering political thinkers in different parts of Africa, such as Fatema Mernissi.

Of course, among the people whom Devaki came to know well was her extraordinarily talented partner—later her husband—Lakshmi Jain. While each lived exceptional lives of their own, together they built an existence larger than the two combined.

This is a most readable account of experiences—attractively recalled and elegantly presented. It is a splendid addition to the literature on the contemporary world.

July 2020

Amartya Sen
Harvard University,
Massachusetts, US

Author's Note

Publishing 'my life' at the age of eighty-seven makes me feel somewhat like Samuel Taylor Coleridge's ancient mariner.*

'*I fear thee, ancient Mariner! I fear thy skinny hand! And thou art long, and lank, and brown, As is the ribbed sea-sand,*' says the young man to a mariner he meets. I have skinny wrinkled hands, white grizzly hair and a wrinkled face. Yes, indeed, writing this story of my life has been like coming off a ship, wrecked by a storm, or out of an ancient cave in the mountainside, as everything that I try to remember seems long ago and yet like yesterday.

A journey spanning seven decades of 'adult' life is certainly a long one. It was natural that there were many waves, storms and stillnesses that I witnessed over those eras and I thought my experiences may reveal some new pictures from the big picture, painted by historians. Persons who may have lived, say, seventy adult years in other periods may find my stories trivial or commonplace but that is in fact the excitement of history. That in some ways it is never new, nor ever old!

**The Rime of the Ancient Mariner* (1798), poem by Samuel Taylor Coleridge.

It is intimidating if not impossible, to even consider writing one's story if one belongs to the era that I belong to—that is the mid-twentieth century. The era was dramatic in many ways—but for us, born in India, it was India's arrival as a free nation as well as a significant one, not only because of the prime ministership of Pandit Jawaharlal Nehru, which left its stamp on the world, but also the ingenuity and charismatic leadership of Mohandas Karamchand Gandhi. How to project what can be called 'my story' in a landscape which was so full of originality, so revolutionary, so full of great characters who walked and scripted the history of free India?

Thus the task that I have undertaken, to write my story, is not only intimidating but even seems ridiculous. Especially since I had no great role to play in this part of India's history. I was more like an ant, while in fact there were many individuals and movements which were like the elephant or the tiger, or a storm.

To describe how one arrived at a particular point in India's social history, where one was considered as a pioneering person in terms of the Indian women's movement, does not seem a significant story. Hundreds of other women—and it continues even today—have made greater contributions than mine to the women's movement as well as to India's political history. So one again is like an ant.

Yet there was a demand that I should write 'my story' and the demand was backed up by a grant to encourage me to write it, and so here I am, writing it.

❁

The desire to put into words and pages everything that happened to me and that I witnessed has been a pull for decades. At the risk of being laughed at, I would even say I wanted to write about my experiences from the time I was a teenager—I began to keep a diary at the age of twelve. Why this desire to write about what one is experiencing? Could it just be ego? Or the love of writing?

The desire got a big push thanks to the extraordinary, unexpected experience of meeting novelist Doris Lessing in London in 1958. I was introduced to Lessing by another writer, Ann Piper. Lessing was at work then on the pioneering novel published as *The Golden Notebook* (1962). Radical in both its form and its politics, it tells the story of a writer, Anna Wulf, who finds she is suffering from a peculiar kind of writer's block. She can still write, but she cannot find a unified narrative that unites all the episodes in her story. Desperate to overcome this block, she buys herself four notebooks, each with a different-coloured cover. The black notebook will tell the story of her life as a writer, the red notebook her political life, the yellow notebook will have her attempts to make 'stories out of my experiences', and the blue notebook will serve as a kind of diary.

This strange division of notebooks helps overcome the initial block, but at the end of this exercise she tries something further. She buys a fifth, golden, notebook, which she hopes will serve to unite the four notebooks. This remains a hope, but the sheer effort of working through her life and her experiences gives her a more valuable insight: a sense of what is, realistically speaking, possible.

My conversation with Lessing lasted for hours, after

which she said to me, 'You must write your story now. Send it to me, I can help you.' I wish I had, but other things—the subject of this memoir—got in the way. Sixty years have passed since I first thought of writing my story. In this time, my self-confidence and my skills as a writer have diminished. I hope no longer for perfection, nor to write my own golden notebook. Instead, I am now thinking of another metal—pittalai, the word for brass in Tamil, the language of my childhood.

In those early decades of the twentieth century, when I was growing up, most of the cooking and the heating of water in the middle-class families of Bangalore and Madras (as Bengaluru and Chennai were then called) was done in large brass utensils, better able than steel to withstand the high temperatures of wood stoves. The interior was treated with some other metal to stop the food from being poisoned by the oxidation process. Brass is a hardier, homelier metal than gold. It represents not perfection or unity, but an honourable imperfection consistent with my own limits. It seemed more appropriate as the receptacle for my story.

On reflection, I think I was born free. I did not only yearn for freedom but seized it, at every chance I got, whatever the grown-ups said: I climbed the tallest trees, went horse riding, did not spend my time merely envying my brothers their bicycles but riding them. I did these things, disregarding the conventions that tried to dictate how girls should behave. While there was much orthodoxy in the family, there was also accommodation. The term used in those days to describe girls like me was 'tomboy'.

I am now proud to say that this 'tomboy' went on to

live her life as a feminist, another way of saying that I lived, to the extent that I could, as a free woman. And to be a free woman, with all its risks and costs, has meaning not just for my public life as a writer, scholar and activist, but my private life of love, friendship, marriage and family.

Looking back, I am almost convinced that freedom, or emancipation from bonds, comes from fighting for freedom, which in itself is the affirmation of freedom.

July 2020 Devaki Jain

New Delhi

PART ONE

Where I Come From

'A woman can walk miles without taking one single step forward. As a child born in a harem, I instinctively knew that to live is to open closed doors. To live is to look outside. To live is to step out. Life is trespassing.'

—Fatema Mernissi

Prologue

I was born in 1933. A year before my birth, my mother had lost a daughter on her first birthday. My aunt and grandmother, both of whom lived with us, said they had never seen my mother so distraught. She was the mother, at the time, of five children. This lost child was, by the standards of the time, extremely attractive, just like my mother. My mother was an outstanding beauty—a delicate, oval face, with eyes large, dark and luminous, long, curved eyelashes, full, pink lips, and long, black hair. This baby had inherited all my mother's best features. She had almond-coloured skin like my mother's, several shades lighter than the normal tan that is most Indians' genetic legacy, a rare and much-valued trait.

Then I came along, light-skinned like my mother, with curly hair and a cheerful disposition. My looks earned me more than the normal amount of care and attention from my father, grandmother and aunt. But my childhood was spent in the shadow of that prenatal loss, of a sister I never had the chance to see. 'She was extraordinary,' my mother used to say, 'not only beautiful but also so lively, so intelligent, so charming, and all this before her first birthday.'

I was the next best thing, but I made the most of the pampering I received. It left me with a sense of self, of my own presence, of confidence, that has enabled me all my life. I was outgoing and fearless; in a word, I was what they used to call a 'sport', game for anything, however unusual or risky.

CHAPTER ONE

An Extraordinary Man

In my story, almost all roads lead to my father, Mandayam Ananthampillai Sreenivasan. Looking back, I marvel at his life and where he reached, given his beginnings.

He wrote his memoirs when he was about eighty-five years old, now my age. *Of the Raj, Maharajas and Me* was the title of the book. We persuaded him to do this as therapy to help him overcome his grief at losing his beloved—my mother—whom he adored. He married her when she was eleven and he was sixteen, but confessed that he felt a passion for her from the moment they met, and he and she sustained that passion all through their lives.

He started his story with the question—who am I? It seemed the right place to start. But he had a trick up his sleeve which, alas, I neither have nor do I have the imagination to conjure up. His answer was to quote from a Sanskrit verse, which shows his ancestry going back to the three great rishis, namely Angirasa, Brihaspathi and Bharadwaja, religious savants of the era of Manu. After showing off that he was a direct descendant of these amazing men, according to the jothishta, the astrologer who wrote up his horoscope, he then pooh-poohs the idea of a genealogical tree, and makes the idea of 'pure' ancestry into a joke. He refers to the various conquests in south India, which might have also led to various kinds of sexual relationships. Thus, generally mocking at the idea of racial purity, extending to pure Brahminhood.

He was born in Madras in 1897. His father worked as an engineer in the public works department of the State of Mysore (now Karnataka). He often told us how when he was in school, he was gripped by the idea of the Sumerian seals, which were apparently being sold in the streets of Madras. He would sell his notebooks which were in demand because he was doing well, and with that money, which would be one rupee or sometimes fifty paise, buy a coin. I remember the coins because he kept them with him for many decades and then gifted them to one of his grandchildren interested in such antiquities.

It is my belief that some persons are born with a spark. I suggest that is the only way their dramatic difference from others who have come from the same background can be explained. This thought, that some persons are inexplicably outstanding within their space, has been incubating in my head for many decades. Looking for illustrations to justify this 'theory', I have found many.

For example, the famous mathematical genius, Srinivasa Ramanujan, was the son of a temple priest, in a highly orthodox Brahmin community, almost a cloister, in Madras. There was no source, teacher, school or book that drove him to develop the extraordinary theorems in mathematics for which he was welcomed at Cambridge University by one of the world's greatest mathematicians, Professor Hardy.

I also think Gandhi was another such genome that

flew out of an unlikely circumstance with shattering ideas. These stars are born with their genius flowing in their veins. I believe my father was born with that spark, otherwise there is no way we can explain his rise. Without any family inheritance of wealth or a relative in public life, he rose to become a cabinet minister in Mysore State and attracted such attention among influential administrators that he was recommended in 1946, at the age of forty-nine, to be the prime minister of the State of Gwalior. In that capacity, he even became a member of independent India's Constituent Assembly—the committee that drafted the formidable, unique Constitution of India.

My father had a very wide range of interests and was more sophisticated than would be indicated by his family background. One time, when he was the mayor of Mysore city, from 1931 to 1933, he invited the eminent, unsurpassed vocalist M.S. Subbulakshmi to the house so that his mother might hear her sing one of her favourite keertanas. This knowledge and appreciation of classical music seems to run in our families, both my mother's and my father's. Inexplicable because neither my mother's mother, nor my father's, went to school, and were married off at the age of seven. But somewhere along the way they learnt how to write in their mother tongues, and of course, the oral tradition gave them access to religious poetry and texts as well as classical music.

As the mayor of Mysore, my father had access to what was happening in the palace. A renowned violinist called T. Chowdiah, who was already one of the palace musicians, brought a young Subbulakshmi—then sixteen or eighteen years old—to perform for the raja. My father was overwhelmed by her music and invited her home, so that his mother may hear her. That started a lifelong friendship, further intensified by the fact that, later, my father joined C. Rajagopalachari in his efforts to build a party called the Swatantra Party. In that effort, Subbulakshmi's husband, K. Sadasivam, and the family that ran *The Hindu* newspaper were also involved.

That strengthened the friendship and brought Sadasivam and Subbulakshmi to our house in Bangalore regularly over the years. They had relatives in Bangalore and it was customary for people in Madras to come to Bangalore in the summer, to escape the heat. So after having the usual coffee, my mother would ask Subbulakshmi if she could sing her a keertana. Subbulakshmi adored my mother—it was a feature of my mother's that she attracted adoration. So a song would be sung. We daughters would sit around and listen in awe.

This was the source of my continued bonding with Subbulakshmi long after my parents passed away. I would visit the couple in Madras and later, after her husband died, she grew even closer to me. She had diabetes, so my husband shared with her his ways of dealing with swollen feet, with diets and so forth. I remember on one occasion, when she was grieving the loss of Sadasivam, she asked me to stay with her and sleep next to her in her bed.

❁

As a cabinet minister in the State of Mysore, my father had to travel on what used to be called 'inspection'. We went on safaris to the forests and wildlife sanctuaries of south India, riding elephants and looking out for tigers. Our clothes had to be khaki or brown to blend in with the natural colours of the forest. Absolute silence was imperative so as not to disturb the animals or warn them of our approach. The elephants, I remember, had a sort of cradle on their backs into which one climbed from a ladder positioned at a slope against the elephant's back. For my mother, they would walk the elephant up to a high platform so that she only needed to climb one or two steps on the ladder.

Sometimes, a forest guard would rush into the guest house in the middle of the night to tell us that a tiger had just been sighted. My father would insist on going on the safari straightaway, and the elephants would be summoned to give us the best possible chance of spotting the tiger. My younger sister, Lakshmi, and I fell in love with elephants; we dreamed of staying back in the forest after the safari and living among these majestic pachyderms.

I have a vivid memory of how the elephant's carer, the mahout, could clamber onto the elephant without the aid of any special devices like ladders. It really was a sight to watch him do it. The mahout would grunt some word that the elephant clearly understood. In response, the elephant would curl the tip of his trunk so that it functioned as a step or foothold. The mahout would climb on that step, and then reach out and hold on to the elephant's ears. Then another grunt, commanding the elephant to straighten his trunk, and raise it up from the ground by about three feet, offering a slope to the mahout, and the mahout would quite literally walk up the slope, still holding on to the elephant's ears and sit astride the elephant's neck!

I was so overwhelmed by this performance that when I was about ten or thereabouts, I begged my father to let me try it. The mahout obliged by giving the command to the elephant. It curved the tip of its trunk in the usual way, offering me the step. I, too, managed to climb up just as the mahout had done, reaching out to hold on to the elephant's ears. I just loved the feat. My father and all the watching forest officers applauded me, and the news spread that I had managed to climb the elephant by its trunk. For a while afterwards, my father showed off my new skill to his friends from Bombay (now Mumbai) or abroad.

The capture and training of young wild elephants was an event in its own right. Elephants were essential to the life of Mysore when it was still a Princely State. They worked in the logging industry, almost like cattle, but they also played a central part in the various festivities in the palace. Princes and images of the gods were always carried on the backs of decorated elephants.

The annual keddah, or trapping of elephants, was an eagerly awaited event everywhere. A pit would be dug and covered with grass and bamboo. Eventually, an elephant would fall into it and be trapped. Then it would be nudged into a barricaded enclosure by an older, already domesticated, elephant. I worried a great deal for the elephants' safety, concerned that they might break a bone or two falling into the pit, but I was always assured, I don't know how truthfully, that the fall never did them any harm. It was still a thrilling occasion: we would all watch from machans, that is, raised bamboo platforms, sometimes even tree-houses, as the elephants were lured towards the trap (this system of trapping elephants has since been banned).

The safari was only one of my father's many passions:

he cared equally for flowers and gardens, for trees, and for sports, particularly tennis and golf. My father loved horses too and taught us how to ride. He loved to swim; the sight of a running stream, while we drove across Mysore State, was enough to make him plunge into it while encouraging us to follow him.

He was what they called the life and soul of the party, and we—my sisters, mother and I—were always included in every part of his life, quite unusual for girls from orthodox Brahmin families growing up in the 1930s and 40s. There was never any suggestion that my mother was any less capable of being adventurous or sporting. She loved it and didn't even let her cumbersome saris get in the way of joining in. But my father, again showing an extraordinarily modern attitude, said she needn't struggle with her sari on the safari and had corduroy trousers and tartan printed shirts made in muted colours for both her and her sister.

But there were many contradictions in my father's character and attitudes, as there were in society as a whole at that time. While he had some very likeable characteristics of modernity, as for example, the way he treated my mother, there was also the contradictory pull of orthodoxy. One of my sisters became a victim of this contrariness in the way he handled her entry into puberty. I think this was partly due to the pressure on him of his sisters and his mother. The power of sisters on men is well known as a phenomenon in India—the formidable bua (in Hindi) or athay (in Tamil). I have never understood the reason for this hierarchy. My father was a tiger usually, but in front of his sisters, he was like a lamb—as my mother would weepingly tell us.

These women alerted my father about the fact that my sister would soon 'come of age', that is to say, have her first period, so not only should that be celebrated but that should be the beginning of a search to get her married.

My sister had her first menstruation when she was thirteen years old and in the tenth standard in her school. It was decided that it was important to celebrate her entry into womanhood. Further, she was polluted according to the custom and, therefore, had to be kept away from everyone else. Thus, as the day of her first period arrived she was put into a room where she was completely isolated. During this period of isolation, it was customary to have someone stay with her, usually a younger woman or an elderly widow. In this case, I was chosen as I was five years younger than her. I was given leave of absence from school and lived with her in the same room for those four nights. Our food was pushed through the door just like they do for prisoners in a jail, and after we ate we would wash our own plates. People would visit and when they did, the door would be opened and they would peer in to see my sister as the person who had attained puberty. We were like animals in a zoo.

A ritual was organized on the fourth day. For this ritual, a function was held to which all the relatives—aunts, uncles and cousins were invited. The community had to be informed that their daughter had now reached womanhood. My sister was decked in flowers from head to waist, and flowers were put around her head almost like a canopy. She was made to sit on a wooden platform and several rituals performed to celebrate her entry into womanhood. After all the rituals were over, she was officially ready for marriage!

While I was too young—eight years old—to feel the pain, for my sister, the experience of being exhibited for something as private as menstruation, was different. She never forgot those painful four days when she was exhibited and, finally, the ritual that was performed when the period was over, and the fact that she could not continue her schooling. She was brilliant, and to her credit it must be said that, despite this handicap, she grew to lead in many spaces—both professionally and at home.

❁

Fortunately, I did not have to go through this ritual—my sister would often say that she was the sacrificial lamb. Strange as it seems, when I look back, my younger sister and I did not get married till we were twenty-eight and thirty-three years old respectively!

This, despite the fact that the process to marry me off had started in 1951, when I was eighteen years old, as I have recorded in my diary. As it happened in the case of my brothers, whose wives were chosen through a process of horoscope matching and other attributes like colour of skin, not so much the level of education, the horoscopes of suitable men were procured from the priests in the temple near our home.

My aunt, Andal, drew up a chart, with the names, ages and educational qualifications of young men who seemed suitable, drawn from within the community. The writings in my diary of the year 1951 provide a glimpse into my torment and confusion.

❁

Diary Notings

April 3, 1951

I believe Anna (my father) got a reply from the father of one of the chosen 'boys'. He is slowly trying to introduce the subject with me. Don't know what do. Andal extols his virtues and I have begun to think too that maybe he is a very nice man...[but I have a] yearning to go to the US, to stay in a school there and have friends. Now I have decided that that's what I ought to do. Maybe the girl who marries this man will be nice and happy and afterwards I will feel regret... maybe not. I'll take the risk, that's all. I don't care.'

April 4, 1951

I have wanted to write a book—'Life with father' type—but now I can't do it for my mind is too full of this entire marriage thing. A day does not dawn without the fear that Anna will call me. So every day is half a torture where one feels scared to see Anna alone, [I] always have to wait for Raja (my pet name for Lakshmi) to accompany me to Anna's room, because then he will not talk about marriage. Oh my God, when will I get peace of mind?

April 21, 1951

I think a letter has arrived from STK (father of the boy in question). He seems to be in a hurry and does not mind if we chuck him up. Big conferences are going on in Andal's room with Chinni (one of my elder brothers), Anna and Akka (my mother). I keep praying for I don't know what.

April 23, 1951

The marriage discussions are getting very hot. I believe Akka and Andal are also in favour of the boy. Should I be too because he is an all-rounder except for one point, looks? Don't know what to do, absolutely harassed. Andal and I are constantly having arguments about this subject…she likes the boy very much and is worried that I will not get a decent husband if I miss this bus. Very frightening at times because it needs piles of courage to face the world alone, above all, the community.

April 28, 1951

Today the discussions are scorching—nothing unusual—since the morning. At night Anna suddenly called me and said he had something to say to me. I guessed right. He told me I had to decide immediately whether I cared for the boy etc. I told him my views, all of course terribly tearfully. He pretended that he wasn't upset. He seems to have told Andal, Akka and Chinni, so they made me sleep in Andal's room last night and tried to persuade me very subtly. They said that they didn't care but I may regret it and so on, all this sounded terribly mean to me. They kept on saying they don't want to force me and all along they were tearing me [apart]. Poor things, it was only their love that made them do that but it hurt. They counted his qualities a hundred times over which made my decision all the more difficult. I don't know what to do. Everything, at times, is so frightening, but at other times it all seems so correct and my decision the best. I'm torn, absolutely, completely; anyway I have done it.

April 29, 1951

This is a very important day in my life. I have taken a decision. God knows whether it is the right one. It may be the turning point of my life. Since I may never get another [boy] as nice so may suffer. Anyway, I have done it. Now I face a dark alley. A thin spark of light can be seen somewhere near the end. Whether it will become brighter and be useful or completely vanish is yet to be seen.

May 22, 1951

Come to think of it, marriage is disgusting in every way, including the real one. Andal hasn't recovered from her disappointment at losing the boy. She talked to Kay (my sister Kaushalya) about it and it made me feel terrible. I'm in a fix, I feel most unsettled. Don't know which road I'm going to take and am just tortured mentally, until I have to break down in the bathroom, with all this talk in the house about the STK boy. Everybody has the feeling that I missed the bus. Feeling low. I could write forever about it and a thousand incidents but right now I'm not up to it.

May 26, 1951

It's my birthday. I turned eighteen today (our birthdays were fixed, not according to the day one was born but according to the lunar calendar). I got up with a feeling of happiness mixed with a fear—fear and a sense of shame—strange? I should think so. It is because I feel that Anna disapproves. If I get over that feeling I would be okay. But somehow it haunts me.

This last noting in the diary affirms my deeply embedded love, admiration and worship of Anna. He was a heroic figure for me, so disobeying him was traumatic. I used to be teased about my love and adoration for him by my sisters not only then, but right up to the time that we were elderly women and my father was ninety-eight years old.

And yet I was the only one who eventually defied him on the question of marriage.

CHAPTER TWO

The Tirupati Princess

I like to think of her as the princess of the hill town of Tirupati.

I call her a princess, as she was considered, even as a child, to be beautiful and charming. Her father, it is said, doted on her. People around their households and in the temple thought there was something divine about her. Her beauty had a certain glow and tranquillity, and beamed love—so she was a great favourite even amongst the temple folk.

If there was any way of interpreting my mother, Akka—it would be as luminous. She was the embodiment of luminosity. 'Akka' means elder sister, in some of the languages of south India. It is said that since her younger sister lived with us, and called her Akka, her firstborn, my brother, Ananth, imitating my aunt, started calling her Akka too, and it trickled down to all of us.

'Bundle of love', her husband called her. Chingu, she was called by her siblings and her mother, a shorter version of Singamma, her given name, which in turn was to give a feminine name to Narasimha, considered a powerful god. This god's name was derived from Simha, the lion. His deeds usually consisted of killing and conquering the evil rakshasas, wicked giants.

She was the second daughter of Singlachar and Yedugiri, and was born in 1903 in Tirupati, a temple town located in Andhra Pradesh. Singlachar was the manager, the peshkar, at the Srinivasa Temple, representing the government of Karnataka. There were two more daughters after her, and a son. Her elder sister, Peri Akka, was married to a criminal lawyer, and had three daughters and a son. The sister after Akka, called Sreerangu, had two daughters and two sons. Then there was one who got tuberculosis and died, and then there was Andal, the youngest, who remained unmarried for a long time.

Akka had seven surviving children. Children were usually born in the house with a midwife or a lady doctor in attendance.

I asked her what it was like to get married as a little girl and have so many children soon after. Bubbling with laughter, she went back to her childhood and said: 'I used to play in the streets in front of our house. We played hopscotch, or kolattam (a form of dance like the dandiya). Tirupati was very hot and humid most of the year. So I would be 'dressed' only in a string around my hips, and the arna kaire. (This was a leaf-size piece of silver, used to cover the private parts).

'Further down the street, there would be young boys playing other street games. I was fair-skinned compared to the other girls, and so the boys would try to reach out to me by jokes and words, from their part of the street.

'There was one boy, who belonged to our caste, whose parents were known to my family, and there was a kind of unspoken signal of love between us. I think he was hoping that we would get engaged when we grew up.'

'As you know,' she continued, 'marriages are finalized

mainly by astrologers; though the initial identification of potential mates for girls or boys is done through relatives and friends.

'My father would travel primarily to Madras where there was a large community of Tamil Brahmins, especially the Iyengar subcaste, and talk to people about potential grooms for his daughters from the pool of young men. In this hunt, he was told about a young man who was doing well in his studies in a college in Bangalore and was the son of a civil engineer who had a government assignment in the city of Mysore.

'My father went to Bangalore to meet this young man and was delighted by him. He said that when he went to the house where this boy was living (the boy was boarding with one of the relatives), he saw a young man who was balancing on a stretch of rope tied between two trees. He was told that this was the young man he was looking for.'

At this point, my mother laughed and said she was glad that her father was not put off. She continued, 'My father was charmed by this interesting young man. He also learned that he was doing extremely well in his studies and would be appearing in the civil service exams for which he was training himself.

'When my father returned, we went to our family astrologer to ask what was in store for me.' The astrologer already had her horoscope and was to compare it with that of the young man, which her father had obtained. But, she said, the astrologer brought out a large plate made of brass in which he poured water. He asked my mother to look into that water and tell him what she saw. She says she saw a man riding on a horse.

The story goes that when finally, this young man was selected to be the husband of my mother and came for his marriage to Tirupati, he travelled by train from Bangalore to the nearest railway station. At the railway station, he got off the compartment and told one of the workmen to open another carriage—and out came a horse. The young man leaped on the horse and rode into the little town of Tirupati, to her father's house, much to the joy and amazement of her father.

Apparently, as a probationer in the Mysore civil service, he had learned to ride and owned a horse as part of his official transport. Recounting this story, my mother laughed and said: 'You see, I had seen him in the plate of water.'

❁

My parents' relationship began on a romantic note and stayed like that over their lifetime together—uncommon among the tradition-bound marriages of that era.

There was a custom that the bride goes to the boy's mother's house for a while after marriage, but not to cohabit. Most times girls like my mother were married before they reached puberty, so this was more an orientation visit. The consummation, a cruel word, often brutally used in those days, had to wait for the girl to have her first period. The boy and girl were not even to touch, till the next ceremony to consummate the marriage which was post-period.

My mother related, with a gleam in her eyes, how when she went to live in her husband's parents' house, she would be asked by his mother to take up a glass of milk for him, just before bedtime. He was studying in a room upstairs for the competitive civil services examinations. And the young man would pull her to him, even though they were not to get physical for another year or so. But she loved it, as she found him handsome and gentle and romantic.

My father remembers those days too. How when she entered he felt her fragrance and embraced her, while she pretended to resist!

Unlike other men of his generation and community, my father encouraged her and took her with him to all his public engagements, parties and travels. Most of his peers would leave their wives at home, because, just like my mother, they did not know much about the 'public' world. But she was his star and he was proud to be with her.

In colonial India, when my father was in government service, the Empire would place a representative in each of the Princely States. In Mysore State, he was called a Resident.

Clubs and parties were part of the culture, and usually, the language spoken was English. The usual mix would be wives of the British officials and some socialites, women and men who were either in business or from the plantations (Mysore State was a coffee-growing area and the British were the main planters).

My father took my mother along with him to these parties, and she remembers how awkward she felt because she did not speak English.

So when we were of school-going age, she admitted us, her daughters, to the convent schools run by Irish Catholic orders, so we would not suffer her handicaps. To do this she had to fight the elders in her family, her mother-in-law and her own husband, as going to a Christian school was considered polluting.

One evening I was sitting with my mother in her home in Bangalore, when she was about seventy years old. I was forty, married with two children and living in Delhi. She had one hour, usually around six in the evening, when she was totally at peace. Just before then, around 5.45 p.m., the housemaid or housekeeper would have given her the key of the storeroom, having put the milk away in the fridge and given out the various rations that the cook would need for the evening meal. The cook would come next and cook dinner. My father would have gone out to play golf around 4.30 p.m. The whole house, particularly the upstairs floor, where my parents' room was, would be quiet and my mother's responsibilities for the day would be over. So, on any given day it was really the first patch of quietness for her.

I used to love asking her about her early days. One story she related has remained in my memory ever since she first told it to me. One of her sons was delivered at home as was the practice in those days. She was sixteen years old. Her mother was with her as the main support, as was the custom. Her mother would look after the baby, his bathing and everything that went into his care. She would bring the baby to my mother only for feeding.

One evening when the baby was brought to her for feeding, she found him looking lifeless. They called her uncle, her mother's brother, who was a doctor. This brother examined the baby and said, sorry, he is dead. It was the middle of the night, so my mother's mother wrapped the baby in a cloth and took him out and laid him on the floor of the cattle shed, behind the house. It was not auspicious to keep a dead body in the house. The households always had cattle and a shed for them where people kept an assortment of things, including bicycles and so on. The baby must have been placed on some straw on the floor.

My mother said she does not remember feeling shock or grief that her baby had been taken away as dead as she had been kept away from the kind of care—bathing, nestling and cuddling—that usually bonds the infant to the mother. Yet, after her mother had gone to sleep and the brother had gone away, she said she crept into the cattle shed to have one last look at her baby. And as she watched him, she found ants crawling over him. So instinctively she tried to brush them off his skin with her finger. The baby stirred at her touch. She rushed back into the house and woke up her mother. Her mother then brought the baby in. Her brother, the doctor, was called back, some medication was given, and she was asked to nurse him. This baby then lived for a good sixty years or more!

This story really shook me. What courage that she could withstand such shocks and carry on with life, and another seven children before she reached the age of thirty-three—of whom again, one died—with insufficient medical care?

I was overwhelmed. There were many more such episodes, revealing a kind of stoicism that Indian women of that era had. My mother-in-law, for instance, lost several children as infants. She remembered how one of them had just fallen off the balcony of an old house in which they lived.

Years later I asked my mother to write her story. Yes, she said, she would like to write about her life. She had been writing amazingly regular newsy letters to all of us, for decades—which means seven children and as many grandchildren! These letters, she often illustrated with crayon drawings. For birthdays it was lights and smiles, for festivals it was a garland of mango leaves and some lamps, and so on.

In the spring of 1983, when she was seventy-nine years old, I was about to go to Harvard University for a semester, to participate in a course on the life of Gandhi. So, I gave her an empty notebook, and pleaded with her to write her story. I also promised to bring her a dictaphone from the US in a few months, so she could just speak out her memories and ideas. She liked the idea, she was eager to write her story.

When I returned after a few months, my mother showed me the notebook, opened at the first page. She had written just one sentence: Naanu ondhu adhrishta shali (I am a lucky woman).

I could not stop myself from asking her, what made her say that? I had seen what a hard and often stressed life she had had. She explained to me how, compared to other women of her generation coming from very orthodox communities and spaces, she was a lucky woman. Her husband, whom she had married at the age of eleven, without any knowledge of his nature, had not only loved her but enabled her to be a partner both in his public as well as personal life. This was unusual in those eras.

Girls like my mother, from orthodox Brahmin families, did not go to school, and if they did it was to the kindergarten. Their education was not taken seriously whereas boys were usually educated and readied for a professional life. These boys, when they became husbands, did not believe that their wives could engage with the educated outside world. So, these wives were screened from any social life, except within the extended families—going to temples, performing rituals. A kind of zenana.

My father was different, even as I witnessed it, as a young girl. He was enamoured by my mother and had great regard for her goodness. In his memoirs, he refers to her as Chingu, the shortened version of Singamma: 'Of story between lovers, I had read in story and song, in poetry and drama. I had thought most of it was romance and poetic imagination. Chingu proved I was wrong. She was sixteen when our first baby arrived. Our sixty-five years together were golden years set with a diamond. Even as pure gold is alloyed to make a jewel, the golden years were not unalloyed with hard times. But when the times seemed dark, the diamond shone with brightness undiminished.'

CHAPTER THREE

Growing up with Father

For a man of his generation, it would have been only normal to have shared certain parts of his life, those involving sport or adventure, exclusively with his sons. But my father was different. He included not only his sons, but also his wife, his wife's mother and sister, and his daughters, into each one of these activities.

One such activity was riding. My love for horses and riding started when I was about four years old. We were living then in a beautiful bungalow in Mysore, called, for reasons I could never understand, 'Bombay House'. In front of the bungalow was a large park in which stood one of the many minor palaces that studded the city of Mysore. Civil servants like my father had, in those days, only horses as their mode of transport. They had to ride when they were away touring the rural areas of the state for 'inspections'. Every morning, a horse would be brought to our house and my father would ride it to work.

Sometimes, he would ask the groom to let me sit on the horse's back and lead it by its reins around the park. They were perhaps the most joyous moments of my day. When I returned from my 'ride', my father would be waiting for me. He would take me down in his arms and say 'Shabash' (well done)!

I learned to ride properly at the horse breeding farm in the village of Hesarghatta outside the city of Bangalore. My father was the minister for agriculture in Mysore State for much of the 1940s and liked to visit the rural parts of the state, particularly to observe how the government's research programmes into modern agricultural techniques or new methods of animal husbandry were shaping up. He would write in advance to have what was called the dak bungalow, built to house visiting officials, reserved for him for the weekend of his visits and instruct them to have three horses, good tall ones, along with their syces or grooms, waiting for him when he arrived in the late morning.

The dak bungalow was a large single-storey building with broad verandahs, a hall and two large bedrooms with beds equipped with mosquito nets, and attached bathrooms. Behind the house was another building that housed a rudimentary kitchen and a room occupied by a caretaker. When my father took his family with him on his trips, it was usually only the women, for my elder brothers by this time were all away at university.

My younger sister and I would dress for riding in breeches made of khaki and hardy shoes. I was, in this and in other things, the bold one, Lakshmi was more nervous and needed to be coaxed. The older women of the party would attend to the food and other comforts. My father would leap onto the horse almost as soon as he reached the dak bungalow. I still needed some help from the syce to mount the horse. The syce would then lead it by the reins behind my father, who rode at a swift trot.

Once we got onto the road, we would turn into the large green fields outside Hesarghatta where my father would speed up to a gallop up and down the slopes, calling out to me to try to ride without the syce's help. It was an exciting moment when I began to be able to trot along with my father without any support, but cantering still made me nervous. One day, he just took the reins of my horse into his own hands and told me to hold tight as he cantered up a long slope, pulling my horse behind him. I was scared at first, then exhilarated. I can remember shouting: 'This is bliss!' My father never forgot my words or the episode and for decades afterwards he would tell the story of how I had felt 'bliss' as I rode up the slopes of Hesarghatta.

Riding remained a passion with me for much of my life. My father's love of horses meant that we continued to keep them long after they had ceased to be his official mode of conveyance. His position as a civil servant was never particularly well paid, but it always came with large official residences with spacious grounds on which it was possible to keep horses and ride. Often, I got to ride myself after he had returned from his own ride around the grounds. Many years later, when I was a student at Oxford, I enrolled in the riding club on the outskirts of the city and would cycle down there for an hour on horseback whenever I could.

❁

I had never imagined that I would end up being an academic and then a research-oriented activist. The dream had been to be a male—sex change is what I wanted when I was twelve years old! Then it was to be a doctor, a neurosurgeon, later a dancer, and then a film star.

This idea of being a brain surgeon had intrigued me since I was ten and I cannot now explain why. I do not remember any role models. But somehow I came to have a feeling that people who had illnesses or difficulties with their brain were the people I would like to heal. This meant that after taking science in the first two years in college, I wanted to join a medical school. Unfortunately, in those days there was no separate college for women to graduate in medicine.

Then that ambition gave way to a burning desire to become a professional dancer, and a secondary interest in becoming an actress. As part of the requirements for grooming daughters for marriage, knowing how to sing Carnatic music was essential. But my most 'out of the box' brother, Sreedhar, introduced the idea of learning Bharatanatyam. I cannot understand how it passed the scrutiny of the elders, but it happened.

One of our relatives, not too close but not too far—my father's mother's cousin's daughter—had fallen prey to the temptations of being a mistress or part of the harem of one of the rajas of the Mysore palace. Then her daughter began to dance and act in cinema and was reputed to be having affairs with other stars. This was a red rag to the rest of the community—'don't teach daughters dancing, they may fall by the wayside.'

But Sreedhar, who had returned from the US with a degree from the Wharton School and modern ideas, could not be stopped. So, a dance teacher was found and my younger sister and I started learning Bharatanatyam. It was exhilarating.

'Thaiyyathai, thaiyyathai,' my dance teacher would call out rhythmically, as I put one foot after the other on the floor. He was unsatisfied with my early efforts. My foot should make a sound when it hit the floor, flat, like a drumbeat. Slowly, I mastered the art of putting my foot down with a slap so that the sound of my feet matched his tappings with a stick on a wooden stool. The rhythm was first slow and manageable but gradually quickened, first doubling then trebling, as I struggled to keep up while also keeping my balance. Even when the rhythm was fastest, I still had to slap the floor with my feet the same way because it was clearly inaudible when I hadn't got it right.

My teacher belonged to the community of devadasis who had historically kept the tradition of Bharatanatyam alive. A big, bulky man, he wore a turban, a white shirt and over it, a European coat. With this, he wore a dhoti that was draped to look like a pair of trousers. He had a heavy black moustache and his lips and teeth showed the marks of his having chewed paan. His voice was gruff, almost as if he had a permanent sore throat.

'Stand straight,' he would say, 'both feet together. Bend your arms to bring your hands to your waist. Now hold it there.' Again the relentless rhythm would start: 'Thaiyyathai...' I was to practise these movements when I was home, he told me. And I did, with great enthusiasm, to the enormous annoyance of my family who did not enjoy my breaking out into sudden fits of slapping my foot noisily on the floor chanting, 'Thaiyyathai...'

The next lessons got more complex and more interesting. One had to alternate with the heel: one, two, three, one, two, three. And so it went on, with me learning to use my feet, then legs and thighs, then the arms, the wrists, the fingers, the neck, even the eye.

Then finally, I was able to do a full 'adavu', the entire sequence of all the basic gestures of the arms and feet that were the building blocks of any choreographed sequence. Eventually, I transitioned from doing the basic exercises to being able to interpret a piece of music into gestures reflecting the meaning of the words and the tone of the lyrics: 'abhinaya'. It was the most extraordinary experience when I could finally do that.

At this time, I met Shanta Rao, one of Bangalore's most respected dancers. She was warm and took to me immediately; I, in my turn, was overwhelmed by her. She was, she told me, putting together a troupe to join her on a dance tour of South America.

I begged her to let me join and tour with them. She watched me dance and saw that I had talent. She taught me for a time, quite unofficially. But when I mentioned to my father that I would like to join her company and travel with her on her South American tour, he refused outright. He went further and said if I defied him and joined her, he would use all his influence in the government to ensure that Shanta Rao's passport was impounded. I had to give up my dream so that Shanta Rao could go to South America!

CHAPTER FOUR

Home as a Nest

I had a full-time guardian, my really safe space—my grandmother.

She was our mother's mother—widowed at the age of forty. Her husband was an official of the State of Tirupati, a guardian of one of the most famous temples in the country, but not wealthy.

She was the daughter of one of the most well-known Ayurvedic shastris, or scholars, in Mysore State. It is said that he handed over his knowledge of indigenous medicine from herbs, roots and leaves to this daughter as she was brighter than his sons. So, she was given the wealth when it came to the wide range of remedies from hair care to face powder to potions for stomach pain and headache as well as post childbirth prescriptions for not only enabling breast milk but for preventing obesity after childbirth, as well as keeping the skin lustrous. She had herbal prescriptions for every kind of ailment, from prevention of diarrhoea to throat and vaginal ailments.

But most of all, she could recite verses from every Indian religious text in two languages—Tamil and Kannada. How could she do that? She got married at the age of seven and never went to school. This was the question that boggled my mind but no one was willing to help me understand.

My grandmother would sit all day with a hand-held fan—a piece of matting affixed to a bamboo stick—fanning herself. She was like a presence watching over me with round dark glasses which hid her fully blind eyes. When she removed the glasses, to bathe or to lie down, one could see white clouds as eyeballs—she had fullblown cataracts in both her eyes. She looked like one of those Chinese good luck gods—the ones that have a big belly and a smile. She was my security, my constant companion, my encouragement and my teacher. Her given name was Yegamma but all of us called her Amma. She was my touchstone—my 'source'. She would sit up nights to keep me company if I had to stay up late preparing for exams. She would inquire after my performance as well as the subject. No one else in the family had time.

Her place was a low wooden bench like a bedstead, with a mattress on top of it and a pillow. It also had two T-shaped stands on either side, on which mosquito nets were strung at night.

When I came back home after a music class, she would ask what particular keertana I had been taught, and as soon as she was told, she would sing it! She had an astounding repertoire of music, poetry and hymns in Tamil and Kannada. She knew lewd songs and wedding songs. She could also recall Sanskrit and Tamil texts. Carnatic keertanas flowed from her mind and there was a throttled, squeezed kind of sound when she sang.

If it was a naughty, bawdy ditty she would start shaking

with laughter, even before she sang it. And when she shook, the bulky body would also shake, her white belly over which hung heavy white breasts. She was very light-skinned, pink almost, strange, as we, her grandchildren, and most of her children, were tan, not pink and cream.

When she lay down, it was always on one side—and then I would have to walk over her legs to relieve pain, a kind of massage. Her legs had so much fat covering the bones that nothing cracked. I held on to the wall next to the bed and, balancing myself by holding on to the wall, I walked over her thighs and legs.

She negotiated her movements perfectly. Holding on to the wall behind the bedstead, she would find her way to a door a few yards away. Then, opening the door, she would feel her way to the next door, which was of the bathroom, do what she needed to do, and negotiate her way back to the bed. She would maneouvre the food into her mouth with the same skill when she had to have her meals. She always sat on the floor despite her bulk and usually ate out of a silver bowl, something that was made for her on a little electric stove in the inner room leading off from our room, or some soaked uncooked lentils on particular days. One of my greatest delights was to sit next to her on the floor, and have her put handfuls of whatever she was eating, into my mouth. The mix, whether it was rice and curds or rice and a soup-like dish, was scrumptious.

❀

My most favourite person in the family, in the trinity of women in my immediate family, was my mother's youngest sister, Andal.

She was my real friend in our jigsaw puzzle household, a saint, a brilliant but overshadowed woman. She was the link, the catch-all, the silent and the unrecognized. The invisible hand that kept all dimensions of the household going, in keeping with her lesser status as an unmarried girl, a non-person who was to be the help for all and sundry. She had no responsibilities either to a spouse or a child—in some ways, a slave to the household.

She remained in our house till she was forty years old, and was our other mother. All her four elder sisters were married, that was their badge for recognition and a conventional journey, so too, her brother. But it was said that she was left behind, as her father died before she came of age, and her mother, as a widow, had neither the presence in society to get this last daughter married nor the means.

She was a living example of unpaid family labour, and this was the pattern for all unmarried daughters or relatives—stigmatized and enslaved. She looked after all of us, our needs when we were in school, the sick and the elderly in the family, the household supplies and so on. She was everywhere and nowhere—grinding the coffee beans, or churning the buttermilk, or enabling her mother to go for her bath, or bringing her brother-in-law his eggs for breakfast—an ever-ready guardian for all of us.

She was the one who ensured the school uniforms were ready, who answered all my queries and sorted out my problems of school, home, hunger, clothes, quarrels. My sisters and brothers teased me, at times hurtfully, because this aunt was partial to me, my shield of protection. I adored her.

All of us, my aunt, my younger sister and my grandmother, shared one room—it was where we slept, and where my sister and I had desks to study.

It was on the second floor, on one side of the house, in a space which was like a kind of alcove. The window was an oblong one, with a lovely glass pane. But grills had been fitted in, made up of fairly close thick wires. This was necessary as birds, squirrels, even monkeys would jump through that window into the room. My desk faced the wall in the front, and on the left at an angle was the window. Behind me against a similar wall sat my younger sister, not always at her desk.

This was my safe place. People in the household left me alone as it was assumed I was studying but actually I was just gazing out of the window.

The view that so distracted me from my studies was a Kundumani tree. It was a tall tree and its upper branches could be seen from my window. In the dry season, very dark, walnut-coloured seed pods broke open and twisted themselves as if they were handmade. Stuck to the inside of these twirls were small red seeds like beads about the size of half a peanut. Looked at from that level, that is, the topmost branches of the tree, these dangling dark brown spirals with bright shining red beads, challenged the imagination with their beauty.

The seeds would fall on the ground and one of the most pleasant games that I played with my cousins—who were a regular feature every evening—was to gather them. They looked like corals though a darker shade.

Some evenings, my mother's sister would come with her daughters and that was my greatest delight. We would rush down to the Kundumani tree and sit there, gather the beads, play with them and talk and talk and talk. We would pierce the beads with needle and thread and make bracelets. We also used them for a game called pallan kulli. In this game, seeds were dropped into sixteen small bowls which were dug into a piece of wood and linked with a hinge.

There were other games which totally preoccupied us. One of the games was with five stones of the size of, say, a strawberry, preferably without sharp edges, but if there were none like that then we would rub the edges on the steps of the house and make them blunt. Better still, when we went to any of the riversides, we would pick smoother stones from the riverbank and save them for this game.

The stones were thrown up and then held with the upper part of the hand or one stone was thrown up and while it was up the other stones were grabbed into the palm—often that failed, and that was the game. Another game was with shells. You had to shake them up in your hand and throw them—the game was to hit one shell with the other, with many variations, and scores were kept, just as in gambling certain formations got more scores than others.

Seven tiles was another game and then gilli dhandu and marbles—all games that could be played in the yard with no special needs for instruments. This engaged us—the girls—for hours, while the boys were out on their bicycles, playing cricket at school or tennis in college. But we had to stay within the 'compound'—and these games seemed to be quite satisfying.

We were seven children: four boys—my brothers, Ananth, Rajan, Parthasarthy and Sreedhar—and three girls, my elder sister, Kaushalya, and younger sister, Lakshmi. I was the one in the middle. Looking back, it may seem strange but we grew up in apparent harmony without experiencing the cruelty of discrimination between boys and girls which is often talked about. Of course, the tradition that girls are to be married and boys educated was strong but it did not seem to be expressed in ways that were felt by us, because the relationship between ourselves, the sisters and brothers, was so close and harmonious.

When the three of us sisters think of our elder brothers, we always remember them as wonderful, caring and supportive men.

Each one of them cared for us in such a natural way, that is, there was no pressure from the parents. It makes me wonder whether this was because of the way my parents ran the home. Our home was such a busy place. My father was very active, deeply engaged in what he did as a person. My mother and the other two women in the house—my grandmother and aunt—were equally busy keeping all the other household activities going. So we grew up without the kind of close mentoring or management that we see in households with fewer children or many middle class households today.

One of my elder brothers, Rajan, was the source of all my literary readings between the ages of twelve to sixteen. The other two, Parthasarthy and Sreedhar, who went to the US for higher studies while I was in college and my younger sister in school, wrote regular letters to us, which kept us up to date with what was happening in those countries, in terms of music, plays and so on. When they visited, they always brought interesting news. They tried to carry us with them—for example, Sreedhar, the youngest of my four brothers and a wonderfully progressive companion, was the one who introduced me to the first ever non-family event that I attended, a seminar in Bangalore run by the Quakers. This then started me on the road of not only an interest in Gandhi and Gandhian ways but also the journey to Ruskin College in Oxford and so forth—which have been some of the most important milestones in my life.

❁

While our brothers were close to us and we did not experience any gender-based discrimination, we three sisters seemed to have had an energy and creativity which was equally spread between us and which made us, in many ways, autonomous.

My elder sister, Kaushalya, who got married when she was very young and had children right away, was perhaps the most capable of the three of us. She created a life of her own which was quite admirable. Fortunately for her, after she had her first child, her husband and she moved to a small industrial town which was built around an English company—John Taylor and Sons. This company was engaged in gold mining and this little town called Kolar Gold Fields was where this activity took place. Hence, it had all the shades of a British community—nice bungalows, clubs and games.

There was a good school also—the usual convent school. My sister engaged with all the club activities, often coming out as a champion, and also enabled her children to study and do well in sports and academics.

When her husband retired and they moved to the bigger city of Bangalore, she found ways of not only keeping herself occupied but also earning an income. Initially, she took up some crafts and later she set up a school for pre-nursery children. She managed this school so brilliantly—by sheer dint of her personality and her deep love for children—that the school became the premier pre-nursery school in Bangalore. Couples particularly sought out her school as the children seemed to become self-confident and capable, and often were able to get entry into what was considered the 'most wanted' schools in Bangalore.

She was in tune with the public space, kept in touch with what was happening and was a personality in her own right. Thus, what could have been a handicap of being married off early while she was in high school did not seem to deter her from being successful and a much-admired citizen of Bangalore.

My younger sister, Lakshmi, not only graduated but also achieved fame in the National Cadet Corps, the youth wing of the Armed Forces that was open to school and college students. She was one of their best, especially in shooting. When she married and had children, she too, developed a commercial activity—a business in handblock-printed silks and cottons in Bangalore. This not only brought her an income, but awards and recognition as well.

I went into academia and then into research. Thus, all three of us, despite having diverse personal lives, were similar in that we were autonomous with our own activities and incomes.

So in that sense, in retrospect, the family and our upbringing, even though it was in the early part of the twentieth century, did not seem to deter any of us girls from either embracing modernity or establishing our own capabilities in the public world.

PART TWO

The Awakening

'If a little dreaming is dangerous, the cure for it is not to dream less, but to dream more, to dream all the time.'

—Marcel Proust

CHAPTER FIVE

The Era That Shaped My Life

I like to call myself and those of us who were young adults in India in the 1950s, *the before midnight's children.* Unlike Salman Rushdie's protagonists who were born at the very midnight hour of August 15, 1947, the moment that India was declared free from British rule, I was born in 1933 and was a teenager at the time of Independence, and a young adult as we threw ourselves into the work of a new and free India. I would say that we experienced an India which we still fantasize about, and which also shaped our politics profoundly. I would go further and suggest that we got deeply attached to some ideas, ideologies and aspirations that were born of that experience that we are not able to shed, even today, in our eighties.

I was fourteen years old when India declared Independence on the fifteenth of August, 1947. I was living in the city of Gwalior in north India, where my father was the dewan of the Gwalior State—the chief minister, in today's parlance. We, his family, were somewhat screened from the turmoil, the agonies as well as celebrations that were going on, especially in New Delhi. But like a new arrow, the assassination of Mahatma Gandhi pierced through our household.

As my father has written in his memoir, *Of the Raj, Maharajas and Me*, a few days prior to the assassination of Gandhi, the assassins had been in his drawing room, angry with him for restricting the activities of the Rashtriya Swayamsevak Sangh or RSS, and also for not including its party members in his cabinet. They had abused Gandhi and amongst others, my father, for supporting the Muslims and made death threats against Gandhi and my father.

My father's term as the dewan of Gwalior ended with the integration of the States into the Republic of India. A Chamber of Princes had been formed, mandated with the task of forging an agreement with the princes to join the Republic. He was engaged as the member secretary of this chamber. That task was also done, so he was getting ready to return to Mysore State. He was commended for having done the job successfully.

Gandhi had heard from Sardar Vallabhbhai Patel, then the home minister, that my father had done well with that task and perhaps wanted to commend him for another government posting. So he had sent for my father and given him an appointment, ironically for January 29, 1948—the day before he was assassinated, January 30.

My father recalls how Gandhi asked him to stay on after the meeting, and pointing to a few people who were agitating outside his chamber, said: 'You see those poor people standing there? They are from Bannu. They have come all the way to see me. One of them was quite angry with me today. He told me, "Gandhiji, you should die." I said I will not die until my inner voice says I should. And do you know, Sreenivasan, what he said?'

Gandhiji raised his hand in a characteristic gesture and said, 'He said "My inner voice says you should die."'

Thus, the very next day when my father heard that Gandhi was shot dead, he was devastated. His conversation with Gandhi on that evening was full of portent and left him and all of us, his family, not only deeply shocked, but politicised.

❁

Until my family moved north to Gwalior, I had little knowledge of the political turmoil in India.

'British bootlicker,' my classmate once shouted at me. We were both schoolgirls, the only two non-Christians in our class at the Sacred Heart Convent in Bangalore. The year was 1942. Our school was at the centre of an area of Bangalore called the Cantonment. It had been built to house British soldiers and other colonial officials. But other communities lived there too—Anglo-Indians, products of mixed marriages, usually between British men and Indian women, converts to Christianity, and Tamil-speaking migrants from the nearby state of Tamil Nadu, brought to the Kannada-speaking city of Bangalore in part so that the British ruling class needn't depend on the local labour supply.

The school was large and had several buildings, mostly made of the famous grey sandstone of the Deccan plateau on which Bangalore stands. Over time, the grey stone had turned a dignified, muddy brown. The house I grew up in too, was built with this stone; it was the most popular building material at the time, easy to maintain because it didn't demand regular painting, and calming in the way it blended with the local flora.

The buildings of my school housed a chapel, a hostel for the nuns as well as one for the students, and classrooms.

The grounds were extensive, with courts for basketball, tennis and other sports. Only the porch was made of cement; the part of it jutting out into the driveway was painted a light blue and had a three-foot niche where stood a lovely statue of the Virgin Mary holding the infant Jesus in her arms.

While most of the other students, largely Anglo-Indian or Goan Christians, would walk or cycle from their nearby homes, my younger sister and I came to school every day, to our great embarrassment, in a coach drawn by a beautiful chestnut brown horse. There were no buses or any form of public transport from where we lived, to the Cantonment. It was like two different cities. We wore the standard school uniform: a blue serge pleated skirt with a white shirt, tucked neatly in, and a brown-and-gold tie with diagonal stripes. We all sang the school anthem—'Brown and Gold'—with great fervour, every morning at assembly.

I loved the various prayers and litanies that were part of the Roman Catholic tradition of the school. I would go to the chapel, make the sign of the cross, sing all the hymns, 'do' the rosary (a friend gave me one to pray with). The rosary had to be hidden when I was at home, and my private devotions restricted to the bathroom. Like so many girls who feel the aesthetic appeal of Catholicism, I wanted more than anything to be a nun. Of course, I breathed nothing of these thoughts to my family at home, upper-caste Hindus who would have been shocked at one of their children abandoning both her family's religion and hopes of a happy domestic life.

As it was, we were not allowed to enter the house proper without first shedding our uniforms, bathing and changing in the bathroom, which we were to enter by the back door. We had two very orthodox grandmothers living with us who regarded close proximity to Christians as polluting.

Out on the streets, nationalist sentiment was growing. The anti-colonial struggle was at its peak. Mahatma Gandhi's call, in 1942, was for the British to 'Quit India'. But almost nothing of that movement resonated inside the house; we were not avid newspaper readers. My father was a civil servant who served the Princely State of Mysore: the State had, since the early nineteenth century, retained a certain measure of independence but at the cost of ceding much of its former power to the British. The Princely States were somewhat cocooned from the nationalist tumult, though in Mysore State, this insulation from politics allowed for a policy of successful industrialisation by a succession of progressively minded rulers guided by extremely competent and far-seeing dewans. Moreover, civil servants in those years tended to stay aloof from the political struggles on the street.

My friend at school came from a business family deeply involved in politics, for it was the commercial (rather than professional) class that was more supportive of the freedom movement. She had grown up in quite a different atmosphere. Politics for her had been the air she breathed. Of course, my family, relatively uninvolved with the freedom struggle, would seem to her like sycophants of the British. To my class fellow, my father's position in the colonial bureaucracy was enough to expose me as a 'toady'. The sense of hurt and humiliation was strong when she taunted me. I wasn't sure what a bootlicker or a toady was, and why I was being accused of betraying my country.

This abuse had come my way because of the enthusiasm with which I had taken part in preparation for a visit by a British school inspector. An enormous map of the world had been brought out, and the students had been asked to colour in red the countries that were colonies of the British Empire and stick little Union Jacks onto them. To go with this was a song called 'The Triumph of the British Empire' hailing the British monarch. I had worked on this map-fixing the whole morning with other students and then learnt and sang the song with such energy that the nuns who taught us, chose me to lead the procession and deliver a speech of welcome to the British school inspector!

All this I had done in perfect innocence, and it was what provoked the abuse from my anti-colonial classmate. It was, effectively, my introduction to politics, to the outside world, and it unsettled me. In a way, the awakening lasted for the rest of my life. I became, and still continue to be, committed to the anti-colonial cause, my sympathies firmly with the countries of the colonized 'South' and my activism concerned with affirming their interests as distinct from those of the old colonial powers. But my journey from the essentially private, bourgeois world of my childhood, to the public struggle that characterised my adult life was long and sometimes tortuous.

❁

Another experience, which took me deeply into the ethos of India's freedom movement, while I was still cocooned in the orthodox family, was a student seminar in Bangalore in 1953. This was convened by the Quakers, in this case the American Friends Service Committee

(AFSC). Normally I would not be allowed to go to such workshops and conferences, but as I have mentioned earlier in this memoir, my brother Sreedhar had me invited. He was studying in the US and was drawn to the spirit and culture of the Quakers.

At the seminar, I was gripped by the simple attire and eclectic ideas of two young men, aged twenty-one and nineteen, who had come all the way from Gandhi's ashram in Wardha—one British, David Hoggett, and the other Indian, Vasant Palshikar. I was fascinated by their attitude, behaviour, clothing and ideas. They were living in Wardha at the Sarva Seva Sangh Ashram. They dressed like Gandhi—that is, dhotis made of khadi, tucked high up between their legs, a light sleeveless banyan, vest, also made of khadi, and coarse handmade leather chappals. They were very calm, friendly and totally at ease with the mixed bag of people that we were.

They spoke about simplicity and identification with the poor. They represented the spirit, the yearning and the effort to usher in Gandhi's idea of the 'second freedom'—freedom from deprivation through sharing with the poor.

I was attracted to them, particularly to David, which led to my first romantic encounter. More of that later.

But looking back, the headiness I felt at the seminar was more than just that of a young romance—it was equally about the new ideas that I had been exposed to. This seminar started me on the road, of not only an interest in Gandhi and the Gandhian ways—but what was to become my political life.

PART THREE

Free to Be

'The only way to deal with an unfree world is to become so absolutely free that your very existence is an act of rebellion.'

—Albert Camus

CHAPTER SIX

Experiencing True Freedom

My first opportunity to step out of the kind of sheltered, cocooned life that girls in families like mine led in those days, was provided by my father in 1955. In the years before Independence, he had served the Princely States in various capacities as a civil servant. After he retired, he was invited, as retired administrators often are, to serve as a director on the boards of various companies. One such position came to him when he was nominated by the Indian government to serve as the government's representative on the board of Air India International—as it was then called—India's only international airline. Once a year, the board met in London and the directors were all flown there at the company's expense. They could bring one companion.

Each year he took one of us from 'the nest'—first my mother, then my aunt, then my elder sister. It was my turn next. He also had another motive, the possibility of my meeting 'a suitable boy', a young man of the right caste, cultured, educated and well-spoken who was doing a PhD in Paris. The meeting, when it happened, was delightful, but I had an uncontrollable desire to go in for higher studies, and experience freedom. I was reluctant to go further with this arrangement. These were not things I could tell my father so bluntly. So when he was due to fly to the US for further engagement, I asked him if I could stay on in London for another week. To my slight surprise, he agreed. He left me money to cover my expenses for a fortnight and introduced me to his friends in the city.

I stayed in a boarding house run by Militza Zernov, a Russian émigré. Her husband, Nicolas, was a scholar of Eastern Orthodox Culture attached to Keble College, Oxford, whom she saw mostly at weekends.

I felt comfortable and happy in London. Notting Hill Gate was the nearest tube station and the area was known for theatre and art. One day, I saw a board announcing a training school for ballet run by Madame Rambert, the legendary Polish woman who came to be known as the Mother of English ballet. I walked in and asked if I could join her class. She made me go through a few stretches, pronounced my body supple, and said I could join. But the fees: ten pounds per lesson! Alas, it was out of my range, otherwise my life may have taken a different trail.

Sreedhar had lived in London before I came there, staying in High Wycombe. At that time, Krishna Menon, who later became Prime Minister Jawaharlal Nehru's key advisor, was a towering presence among Indians in London, having founded the India League to campaign for the country's independence. It had a small office on the Strand.

Menon was known for encouraging young Indians who came to London. He befriended my brother, who was outgoing and intelligent, and also introduced him to Vijaya Lakshmi Pandit, who was the high commissioner of India in London. Sreedhar wrote to Krishna Menon about my desire for higher studies and asked me to call on him. I visited Menon at the office of the India League on the Strand. Menon was friendly and quite unencumbered by the fact that he was such a prominent figure in India's politics. He tried to help me; he spoke to the officer in charge of education at the Indian high commission, a Mr Kashyap, to seek a place for me in any university in the UK.

Mr Kashyap could not find a place for me, the admissions were all over by August, but he invited me to his home for a Sunday lunch where I met Harindranath Chattopadhyay, the famous poet and actor-brother of Sarojini Naidu, one of the most prominent figures of the Indian freedom struggle. It was not a pleasant afternoon, as Harindranath was a predator, holding me close to him as we stood to take a photograph, letting his hands play over my back, all entirely new experiences for me. This aspect of his character has been confirmed in anecdotes about him in various biographies, including that of Kamaladevi Chattopadhyay who was married to him for a short while.

Sreedhar also wrote to Mrs Pandit. When he told her that I was in London, she invited me to an official reception that she was hosting in her house. Triloki Nath Kaul, known as Tikki Kaul, was at that time the deputy high commissioner. He received me when I walked into the reception and led me to a graceful woman with a big warm smile and well-groomed white hair. She first shook my hand and then embraced me. She asked me what I was doing, where I was staying, what were my plans in London.

Happy to have the attention, I told her everything, including my problems and challenges. She laughed and said, 'Would you like to come and stay with me for a few days?' I was stunned but quite happy to do that. I moved in with Mrs Pandit.

One day, she asked me if I had a good portrait of myself—I could not understand why but when I said no, she decided I should be photographed. She called one of her secretaries and the next thing I knew, I was being driven in a car belonging to the high commissioner to perhaps one of the best photographic studios in London. While I much enjoyed staying in the luxury of the Indian high commissioner's house, I chose to move back to my boarding house soon after.

While in London, I had been told of a two-week seminar, once again organized by the Quakers, which was to take place in Saarbrücken, Germany. Those selected would not have to bear any costs. I decided to go for it and took the ferry across the English Channel and a train followed by a bus to the site. The last lap, on the bus, was the first time I felt any fear. The bus was full of miners on their way home. I was in a sari and had a long plait and must have looked as helpless and frightened as I felt, clutching my small attaché. The men stared and laughed. Nothing happened, nobody hurt me, but for much of the journey I was convinced I was in serious danger.

I got off the bus, following the instructions, and walked for about two kilometres to the house in which the camp was to be held. The camp, which had both men and women living under the same roof, was perhaps my first strike at freedom. During the day we met to discuss many topics, sharing our life histories and ambitions. But in the evenings after supper, in a natural kind of way, the girls and boys began to pair off, taking walks in the woods alongside the house. My partner was a Yugoslav, Vojin Dmitrivitch, and the woods were just right for passion—I fell in love with Vojin.

At that camp I also met a young Dane, nineteen years old, and planning to be a veterinarian, who taught me to hitchhike. When he heard that I was going back to England, he said: 'Why don't you come with me? I am also going to England but will be hitchhiking. I will go from here up north through Germany and up to my home which is in Copenhagen and then I will be going back all the way to England, via Sweden. It will cost you nothing.' I promptly agreed and had my first most wonderful experience of Scandinavian beaches and hitchhiking.

When the seminar was done, we hitchhiked our way to Frankfurt. He knew all about the free youth hostels that were dotted all across Europe and we would stay there for the night. The next morning, we would make our way to the main road and continue our journey. We went to the beaches in Denmark and Sweden as it was summertime. I can never forget my first experience of coming out in a bathing suit onto a beach. Girls were given cubicles where they could change. I found it unbearably hard to emerge from the cubicle with nothing on but a bathing suit. To this day that young man, who is now a retired veterinarian, teases me for my extreme inhibition. For one month we were on the road. Finally, we hitchhiked back to London.

I did not want to go back to India yet. But how could I negotiate my stay? One of the boarders at the 'house' advised me to go to the employment exchange in London. It was the 1950s and citizens of countries in the Commonwealth were eligible to work in the UK with none of the restrictions they have to face today. The exchange found me a clerical job at five pounds ten per week. The boarding house charged three pounds per week without breakfast, so the rest went for the tube and some food.

Looking back, it is surprising how little my father resisted when I said I'd like to stay on in England and try to enter a university. He not only took it very well but even spoke to a friend of his—a diplomat at the Indian high commission—to ask if he could help me find admission in a suitable course.

But any old course would not do. I had set my heart on Oxford. It is an extraordinary thing to admit, but Oxford meant nothing to me when my landlady in London, Militza Zernov, first mentioned it. I could not remember anyone mentioning these famous universities—Cambridge and Oxford—when I was growing up, neither at home nor in my college. My landlady was shocked when she found that the name and place meant nothing to me. So she took me with her when she drove to Oxford to attend the annual reception at Keble College, a garden party hosted by the Alliance Française.

The first sight of that city enthralled me. I was stunned by the architecture, the Gothic towers, and the students cycling down the streets with bags full of books and black coats flying. It was seductive. I was seized with a determination that I must get there.

Another chance remark showed me the way. The University of Oxford itself was impossible to get into—it was June and admissions decisions are made at the end of the previous year—but the city had another institution that might have me.

This was Ruskin College, an institution founded at the end of the nineteenth century by American reformers inspired—as Gandhi had been—by the writings of the social critic, John Ruskin. It was not one of the colleges that make up the University of Oxford, certainly not one of the ancient colleges that had first caught my eye. Its students were much older and came, not from one of the old public (that is private) schools that educated the British upper middle class, but from the ranks of the working class. The subjects it offered were not Greek or Latin, but economics and industrial relations. I wrote to the college seeking an appointment. To my surprise, they granted me one, even though this was August and they had finished their admissions process for the coming academic year. I was called for an interview.

Was I a worker? the principal asked me. 'Not really,' I said. Had I ever been in a trade union? Again I had to say no. Did I know this was a labour college? Yes, I said, but I just have to be admitted, I want to be in Oxford. Did I have financial support? None, I admitted. Inexplicably, he admitted me with a full scholarship, tuition fees and boarding and lodging for one year.

Many years later, I had the chance to ask the principal, Mr H.D. Hughes, why he let me in. Pure amusement, he said, at the sight of this evidently upper-class Indian girl in her early twenties, asking desperately to be allowed to study alongside men and women in their thirties with more than ten years of hard manual labour behind them. How, he said, could he resist such a social experiment? Besides, he added, he had felt moved at the desperation he could feel in me, to study in the atmosphere of Oxford. He felt that I would put it to good use.

Hostel facilities were minimal at Ruskin. We were eight women and maybe thirty-five men—all above thirty going up to fifty years of age. A large room, with four washbasins, one tub and a few cubicles with commodes was our space for cleaning ourselves. There were no showers and I recall my consternation that I had to wash my hair, at that time long, in the washbasin—as all the other women did. There was no way at Ruskin of washing it as I was accustomed to do in India: allowing it to soak all the way through in the running water of a tap or pouring water on it with a mug from a full bucket.

A fellow student came to the rescue. Jean Rossiter's mother had been a 'char', a woman who cleaned floors and did the dishes at houses and offices, her father a carpenter. She had grown up in Tottenham in north London, a neglected working-class neighbourhood. She had shown academic promise when working as a secretary and received a Workers' Education Council Scholarship to get a diploma at Ruskin College. Jean saw me struggling and showed me how she did it: bending over the sink and letting the cold water run over her head. It was a terrible method, uncomfortable and inefficient. My hair was two feet long. It was impossible to wash it without spilling water all over the bathroom floor. But Jean's unfussy, pragmatic attitude to the whole thing taught me not to make a fuss.

I was the youngest in my class at Ruskin. No one had come here straight from school. They were full-time workers who had been selected from those who attended the special classes conducted by the government for workers, for further education. They had modest scholarships, with no money to eat out or order wine, as the middle-class undergraduates at the 'main' colleges of Oxford University did. If you were prudent during the week, there might be some money left over to buy beer on Saturday. I was in a worse fix. The college had given me room and board and tuition free, but no cash. And I had none.

How to manage during the vacations for room and food? I decided to work during the vacations in a café called Cadena Café on Broad Street (demolished in 1970). It was very popular amongst the undergraduates. The café had put up a 'Wanted' board for a dishwasher. I applied and got the job. There would be some cash per wash and some meat with mashed potato after the dishwashing. The Zernovs also attended a chapel for the Russian Orthodox Community in Oxford. This chapel was housed in a building on Canterbury Road, and let out some rooms. I took one, paying out of the wage I earned for the dishwashing.

My own perceptions changed over the course of that year. I came to regard posh undergraduates as affected fops, dandies with effete accents and absurd umbrellas. The most ridiculous or laughable of these were the Indian men dressed in waist-coated suits, carrying umbrellas and talking with the stuffy, huff-huff accents of the public school students.

My comrades at Ruskin were all from the working class. I wanted nothing more than to be one of them. I accompanied them to the pubs on Saturdays. I drank beer and learnt how to smoke a pipe. I ate what was provided by the college kitchen—bread often accompanied by bacon or sausages, lunch with overboiled vegetables, even beef—sometimes raw granules, made into a kind of mound—if that's all there was to eat. We just had to satisfy our hunger from that kitchen; there was no money to eat out.

Ruskin College and its atmosphere was not only political but deeply associated with anti-colonialism. It supported the freedom struggles in the colonies. The college supported men and women from the colonies, to access education in the UK. Thus, Tom Mboya, who later played a significant role in Kenya's struggles for freedom and became a cabinet minister, was also a student during my time. We veered towards each other naturally, two foreign students from the colonies. Being with Tom was my first education on colonial struggles, racism and the revolutionary spirit of young persons in the colonies. On Saturday evenings, when there was a regular dance with recorded music in the Hall in Headington where the college housed its first year students, Tom and I paired naturally.

Tom remained a friend even after we graduated and left Oxford. He invited us, my husband Lakshmi and I, to his inauguration in Nairobi. We both went, and Tom then spent time with Lakshmi explaining the challenges they were facing in Kenya. It was an irrevocable blow to Kenya that he was murdered.

❁

David Hoggett, the Englishman whom I had met in Bangalore in 1953,who had lived in India as a volunteer and adopted Gandhi as his model, had returned to England. He was engaged with the Campaign for

Nuclear Disarmament led by Bertrand Russell. I rode on his motorbike to join the thousands protesting against nuclear weapons in Trafalgar Square in 1960.

The men and women at Ruskin were some of the most liberated people I had ever met even though they came from the real working class. For example, we had a former postman from Ireland, a worker in a mine from Yorkshire, typists from north London, where communities named the Cockneys lived. My best friend, Jean Rossiter—someone whose friendship lasted till 2017 when she died—took me home to Tottenham for Christmas. Another fellow student took me home to Yorkshire for another of the breaks. His father was a coal miner.

Neither of these families had ever been near a person of colour. Yet each family embraced me, took me into their hearts. I went to a pub in Yorkshire where again the men were delighted with my presence and I drank more beer, toasted by them, than normal.

The inclusion by the students was particularly extraordinary, considering that they had not ever socialised with a non-white person. At the most affectionate, they would call me 'wog'(a person who is not white). 'Let's take the wog out for a drive'—so the postman student took me to the countryside and showed me the first primroses as they emerge after winter. I was so enthralled by that sight.

Ruskin College's deep association with labour and anti-colonialism left an invisible kind of awareness in me—first, about workers and trade unionism, and second, about imperialism and global politics. But what was most striking in terms of an experience was that I did not have to be accountable to anybody for any action: where I went, who I met, how long I stayed out. Nothing!

The skill that I had picked up on the trip to Germany served me in good stead. Hitchhiking seemed to be such a simple, easy way of travelling without incurring any expenditure that I began to use it for my travels within England. If I had to go to London I would hitchhike; if I had to go to Ireland I would hitchhike up to the coast and then to the village in Ireland, where I went for a week's holiday. Wherever I went, I always wore a sari. My fellow students from India were appalled at the thought. One of them, Yashodhara Sengupta, a cousin of Amartya Sen, later Yashodhara Bagchi, recalls how she was inculcated into hitchhiking by me and what a thrilling experience it was.

Maybe we were just lucky then, but it seems to me that there was a time when the kind of assault on women that one hears of now, was not as easy as it has become since then. A girl in a sari could hitchhike from Oxford to Edinburgh and not have a single experience of sexual assault. I do not think anyone today can count on having such an experience.

CHAPTER SEVEN

Engaging with India

On my return from Oxford in 1956, at home there was the usual question of getting married. I was way past the regular marriageable age. My elder sister was married when she was fifteen; and my brothers, at the ages of twenty-three and twenty-four, married girls who were seventeen or eighteen, with the conventional six or eight years age gap. I was twenty-three years old.

I pleaded with my father that I would like to work and have a professional job for just a little while before I jumped into marriage. It surprises and pleases me to recall that not only did he agree, he even helped me by introducing me to a friend of his, Minoo Masani.

A Parsi and a patriot, Masani was an employee of the Tata family of industrialists. He was looking for an assistant to help him to write a book which would lay out an economic programme for India which, as he put it, was neither American capitalism nor Soviet communism.

Under Nehru, India had adopted what was called a 'mixed economy' with the state taking the lead on development by establishing many public sector enterprises like the Bharat Heavy Electrical Limited (BHEL), Hindustan Aeronautics Limited (HAL) and so on.

Many leaders of the Congress who had engaged in the freedom struggle alongside Nehru, were not in favour of the state taking over so much of the economy. Among them was C. Rajagopalachari, one of the most prominent political leaders from the south of India and also the first governor-general of India. These persons along with Minoo Masani, Achyut Patwardhan and other members of the Congress Socialist Party, founded in 1934 a group within the Congress. They were concerned with the overwhelming dependence on the Soviet Union, not just for economic development but also in terms of India's political alignment.

These leaders went on to create the Swatantra Party, literally the Freedom Party. My father, who had kept his distance from politics as a civil servant, in his retirement years went on to embrace political life as one of the founder members of the Swatantra Party. They brought out a paper called *Freedom First* and established an agency called the 'Forum of Free Enterprise'. *Freedom First* was edited by Minoo Masani and my father wrote a regular column in it.

Masani also ran a small research organization in Bombay, called the Democratic Research Services (DRS). He hired me to work as his assistant at this organization for a salary of Rs 300 per month. It was a small office and the only other companion I had was a young Parsi woman, a typist called Roshan. For somebody who had never been to Bombay, it all seemed so easy and simple to be working in that city. I had never stepped out of my hometown, Bangalore, to live in any other city in India.

A cousin found a bed for me in a Roman Catholic hostel called Villa Teresa, on Peddar Road in the busy southern part of Bombay. I shared my room with three others and we all slept on bunk beds. Considering that I was being paid Rs 300 per month, to find a room which gave lodging and breakfast for Rs 150 was really a gift. I would walk down to the nearby Kemp's Circle every weekday morning and catch the bus to Masani's office at Churchgate.

❁

It was while waiting at the bus stop one morning that I made a wonderful new friend. A large car passed by me, then slowed down, and the woman driving it called out: 'Are you Sreedhar's sister?'

'Yes,' I said.

'Jump into the car,' she said.

I jumped in without a second thought. This woman was the economic historian, Dharma Kumar, one of the most intelligent and charismatic women I have ever known. She was working at the Reserve Bank of India in Bombay at the time and, I learnt, had known Sreedhar from the time that he had worked as a manager in a large construction company in Delhi. Her husband, Lovraj Kumar, worked for Shell and the couple lived in an apartment further up on Peddar Road.

She more or less adopted me while I lived in Bombay. 'Why don't you come over home after work,' she said. 'Even if I'm not there, my daughter will be there with the woman who looks after her.' This daughter, Radha, a graduate from Cambridge, evolved to become a specialist in political conflict resolution, worked in Eastern Europe and returned to India to lead the Nelson Mandela Centre for Conflict at the Jamia Millia University. Much later she was one of the interlocuters who were appointed by the government in an attempt to resolve the conflict in Kashmir.

Naturally, I agreed. Their large apartment was so much nicer than my poky hostel room. Dharma absorbed me into her household as well as all her extracurricular activities like driving to the beach in Manori with other intellectuals like Maurice and Taya Zinkin. Taya Zinkin was the *Guardian's* correspondent in India. Every now and then, Dharma would take me along when she went to her mother's house in Matunga, where we would have 'oil baths' in the traditional Tamil way. That is, we would smear gingelly oil on our bodies, then scrub it off with a rough powder, also made out of ground seed pods, cheeka, and pour warm water over ourselves. Dharma loved these baths. So did I.

Dharma also introduced me to Oxbridge folk in Bombay, amongst whom was a young man, Foy Nissen, also 'Cambridge returned', who was working in the British Council Library. He had a scooter, a Vespa which was just beginning its entry into urban India. We became friends. He would pick me up after work, I would sit astride on the pillion (always in a sari, the salwar kameez had not taken over India at that time), and we would drive through the city, to the seaside. Eyes would pop as we stopped at traffic lights, as the scooter, especially with a woman riding astride, was still an uncommon sight. Once we drove out to a Gandhi ashram, four hours away, and much to the annoyance of the severe head of the ashram, slept in his verandah. Other times we would drive to the ocean and sit leaning against the rocks—completely beautiful and enthralling experiences. Foy brought me books, and introduced me to wonderful poets. One who gripped me is Alun Lewis, whose heartrending poem I use in this book. We fell in love and he came to Bangalore, to persuade me to marry him. But that was not part of my plan.

The Roman Catholic hostel gradually became a place where I would only go at night to sleep. My days were filled with work and friends and all manner of interesting activities.

❁

When the draft of the slim book was ready, Masani had it printed and called it *The Democratic Alternative*. It strove to find an economic path for India away from the prevailing dogmas—it proposed, for instance, cooperative farming as a more viable alternative than the collective farming championed by the Left, which the Right opposed on the ground of individual property rights. It proposed strengthening small-scale industries, and so on.

Masani arranged for its release at an event in Varanasi in 1957 by no less a personage than Jayaprakash Narayan, a Gandhian and political stalwart who was greatly respected for his independence of thought.

There I was, on my first trip to Varanasi, under a big tent with about 200–300 people and J.P. Narayan on the podium with Achyut Patwardhan and Rukmini Devi Arundale. She was a formidable leader—a theosphist who had set up Kalakshetra, the academy for Bharatanatyam at Adyar, near Madras, and became the first woman member of the Rajya Sabha.

On stage, I was introduced as the author of the monograph and I read from it standing behind a microphone. It was the first time for me. Happily for me, the little book was not only much appreciated but there was great astonishment that a young woman should have prepared such a well-founded political economy document. The reading was followed by a debate on the book.

After the event, Rukmini Devi sent for me. She seemed to be overwhelmed by the fact that I was also from south India, a Tamil like herself. She invited me to go on a cruise along the Ganga in one of the most beautiful boats that I have ever seen, a large boat with a canopy, sofa-like chairs where she sat like a queen, and we drifted along the river in regal style.

❁

On completing the three-month assignment with Minoo Masani, I started looking for another job. I was particularly interested in a job that would involve me with the cooperative movement. The cooperative was an alternative to both the state and the private sector, and seemed like a promising place to carve out an ideological space that was neither capitalist nor (in the Soviet sense) socialist. In the course of my research, I learnt that the Indian Cooperative Union (ICU) in Delhi was setting up a research division, and was looking for a research assistant. I applied, and was interviewed for the position. I was offered the job which I accepted without hesitation. I would now be moving to Delhi.

To my delight, shortly after, Dharma and Lovi also moved to Delhi, and we kept up our friendship. They would often invite me to dinner at their house on Pandara Road. Their drawing room was a remarkable place.

On any given evening, the best scholars, intellectuals, journalists and writers of the age could be found there, discussing books and the current political scenario.

Dharma was at the centre of it all. She was a voracious reader and always had something to say, about novels and poetry as well as about her own intellectual specialism, economics and the social sciences. She had already acquired a reputation as a formidable conversationalist in Cambridge: quick-witted, engaging and impossible to patronise. A widely circulated anecdote from her Cambridge years captures something of this quality. Apparently a Cambridge don at a party had said, quite unaware of the ridiculousness of the remark, that 'time is just a device to stop everything from happening simultaneously.' To which she replied, quick as a flash, 'Then I suppose space is just a device to stop everything from happening in Cambridge.'

Her conversations in Delhi had the same quicksilver quality. Surrounded by other people who were close to being her intellectual equals, she came into her own as a hostess, thriving on the clever, intense engagement with intelligent men and women. There were scenes straight out of Simone de Beauvoir's novel about French intellectuals after the war, *The Mandarins*.

I can remember some of the figures who used to frequent that drawing room. Amongst them were Romesh and Raj Thapar, who managed the influential journal, *Seminar*. My brother Sreedhar, representing a steel industry consultancy, and Pitambar Pant, then in the Planning Commission, would often be there too. Some of the regulars lived on Pandara Road and some in Chanakyapuri: my brother used to call them the

Panchampali group. There were others too in the circle: V.K. Ramaswamy, Aparna Basu (then Aparna Mehta) and Andre Beteille—all from Cambridge.

The heroine of the group, I think, was the luminous scholar, Sita Narasimhan. She had studied English at Cambridge and the others regarded her as the most impressive intellect of them all. She did not live in Delhi, for she had stayed on in Cambridge and when she was in India, she tended to be with her family in Madras. But on her trips to Delhi, she was lionised by the others. Dharma, in particular, adored and revered her.

One episode from those years has stayed in my mind, perhaps because it revealed something of my own place in the group. I had a similar Oxbridge background and had an academic position, but I did not regard myself as equal to them in sophistication. One evening, I can remember all of us sitting on a carpeted floor with our backs to the wall in V.K. Ramaswamy's father's house. His father had the rank of a minister, being deputy chairman of the Planning Commission of which Nehru was the chair. Someone said, with considerable excitement, that Amartya Sen would be joining us.

Even to those who didn't know him personally, Amartya Sen, even as a young man in his twenties, was a charismatic figure. It was clear to everyone, even those who had only known him as an undergraduate, that he was one of the great minds of his generation. Great things were expected of him, and when he won the Nobel Prize for Economics several decades later, none of us was in the least bit surprised. Sen was also known to be a Marxist.

Amartya walked in dressed in the Bengali style, in a dhoti, kurta and a shawl. He was a beautiful man. The conversation turned very quickly to ideas like Marxism. The room was full of people who were not themselves card-carrying Marxists but progressives. I was a little frustrated with the direction of the conversation, unsure exactly what it was that Amartya was supposed to be. Quite innocently, I decided to ask him: 'Amartya, what is Marxism?' There was shocked silence in the room but I was too raw then to notice the effect my question had had. Amartya, to his credit, took the question entirely in his stride, and answered it in his characteristic way: erudite and clear. Later in the evening, Amartya asked if I ever visited Calcutta (now Kolkata), where he was living at the time, and said I should let him know if I did. We became friends—a friendship that has lasted all these years.

❀

At the Indian Cooperative Union, we were encouraged to work in the field and collect data on cooperatives and rural workers. I asked to be allowed to learn by participating in the 'bhoodan' movement. This was an idea that was developed by Vinoba Bhave, a disciple of Mahatma Gandhi, as an illustration, or a follow-up of Gandhi's idea of rural reconstruction. He appealed to large landowners to voluntarily give some of their land to the landless. 'Bhoodan' literally meant the gift of land. I was so impressed by this idea of appealing to human goodness, that I felt that if I was truly attracted, I would even walk with Vinoba Bhave across India in his endeavour to redistribute land, from the landed to the landless.

There was idealism everywhere—one could not be

a young person, whether one was a college teacher or a researcher, without wanting to jump into some river which was about rehabilitating or reconstructing India, post-freedom.

I arrived at Vinoba's camp in a part of Maharashtra that I cannot remember. Everyone was busy either preparing for the march or preparing to distribute food. It was impossible to meet Vinoba.

By 9.30 p.m., people were dead tired and we were asked to sleep. I had not carried anything except a rug and a sheet. There was a large wooden platform in the camp, raised a few feet above the ground, with pillars on all four sides supporting a roof—a common feature of villages, where one could have a discussion during the day, or a wedding or a puja—or stretch out for the night. So, spreading my rug on this big open platform, I fell asleep.

I was woken up at three in the morning when it was still dark, and told to get ready which meant, finish your ablutions. So off we went to the bushes to relieve ourselves. There was just one tap behind the platform where we could wash ourselves, and so two women would go together, one would hold a sari as a screen, while the other quickly poured some water on herself. I followed the drill. We were given some gruel and tea. Then strapping whatever baggage we had to our backs or carrying it on our shoulders, we set off to walk to the next village. It was about 4 a.m., still dark but cool. Lanterns were carried by one or two persons in the front and in the middle of the procession. The walk was about eleven kilometres.

I moved up the crowd on the march and introduced

myself to Vinoba with a namaste. I spoke in English and told him I was studying the various forms of rural development in India and wanted to learn about this idea of the giving of land voluntarily in a village.

In Hindi, he asked, 'Where are you from?' When I said that I was from Karnataka, he started speaking to me in Kannada. I told him I could not speak well in Kannada. He turned to me and said, 'What language can you speak?' I said English. Instead of getting angry, he laughed and said, 'Doesn't matter, I will speak to you in English. What do you want to know?' I asked him what his hopes were, what would he like me to do, and insisted that I wanted to participate in the work. He arranged for me to meet his colleague who handled the post-walk development activity. That gentleman, Anna Sahib Sahasrabudhe, directed me to go to Orissa and live in a village called Jharigaon in Koraput district, which had actually engaged itself in 'gramdan', which was one step ahead of bhoodan. Here the ownership of land by individuals was collectively vested in the village.

I was to live there and help the local community to reconstruct their area and develop it as a collective.

I went back to Delhi, got permission and support from the ICU, and then took a train to Calcutta, en route to the village in Orissa. Those days, the trains had a special compartment for women and I had booked a sleeping berth. It was rare for a woman to travel alone. The compartment would be full of women travelling in a group, often with their children. As soon as I boarded the train, the women started assailing me with questions: was I married, did I have children, they asked. When I said I was single, they abused me, and asked me to vacate my berth for other, more deserving women—a young mother feeding her infant, or a pregnant woman who needed to rest.

From Calcutta, I took a bus to Koraput. Letters had been written to the man in charge of the little ashram in Jharigaon village. He turned out to be a graduate from Oxford. His name was Nagin Parekh and he came from a wealthy Parekh family in Bombay. But he had also been smitten by idealism and decided to give his life to village work. We talked and we shared whatever food we had. He spread out two mats on the floor and we both slept in his little cottage. Next morning, he took me to see the villages and I took down notes.

It was an extraordinary experience of observing voluntary contributions towards equality. It seemed a brilliant way of ushering in a more equitable distribution of wealth. I stayed with him for a week.

On the way back, I stopped at Calcutta. While I was there, I stayed with my friend Amlan Dutta, a socialist I had met while I was working at the ICU in Delhi. I wrote to Amartya to tell him I was in Calcutta, staying with Amlan. He was mildly surprised, or perhaps impressed, at the nonchalance with which I, an unmarried woman, was willing to stay with Amlan, an unmarried man. In fact, it was not particularly astonishing: it was just how things went in social movements. It was part of their unorthodox culture of solidarity.

Amartya came around to the flat to pick me up and took me to, what was for him and other intellectuals of his generation, the cultural centre of the city: the

Coffee House. He had assembled his friends there to meet me. Among them was Andre Beteille, who became one of the most important social anthropologists of his generation, and Jacques Sassoon, who became a disciple of Balamuralikrishna, a famous vocalist from the Carnatic tradition of classical music. They all wanted desperately to hear me talk about Vinoba Bhave and his movement: was it real? Was altruism working? What a thought!

I had to refuse. I was unsure about the attitude they would take to Gandhian movements. Their politics had been shaped by Western ideologies, and they were sharp intellects and articulate debaters. I felt, I now think wisely, that I needed a good deal more experience and reflection before I would be ready to describe and defend the movement to such interlocutors. I directed the conversation to lighter topics. We had a wonderful day, laughing and talking and getting to know each other as people rather than as ideologues or intellectuals. Amartya then took me for a drive through Calcutta, as it was my first visit to that city. I said I wanted to eat Bengali food. I remember we went hunting for such a place and finally he gave up.

These travels of mine, which were getting me further and further away from marriage, thankfully did not create a storm in the family. Everyone seems to have been busy and I was also following a road without too many obstacles.

CHAPTER EIGHT

Falling in Love: The Unsuitable Boy

'Are you listening?' I said. 'I love you. You have to marry me.'

'You know I'm engaged.'

'Yes, I do! But you must break it. Because I love you.'

❁

He was a beautiful man, with clear, glowing skin, luminous eyes and full, sensual lips. He wasn't tall, but wasn't short either, and well-built. He spoke softly, but with the confidence and passion of an instinctive leader, in full command of himself, his mind and the organization he served. It was 1957; he was thirty-two, I was twenty-four.

❁

We were living in an age when the name and philosophy of Gandhi meant something: for most of us, he was still part of living memory. The ideals of his movement and the moral authority of his personality gave him a power that went beyond anything possessed by any living politician. It is difficult to explain this to people who have grown up in subsequent generations, to whom he is a historical figure. The idea of a Gandhian social activist had an attraction that gave everything associated with it a strange romance: the austerity of the lifestyle, the deep concern with truthfulness and personal integrity, even the bush shirt and trousers made of homespun khadi cloth.

Lakshmi Jain—that was his name—was what we called a 'constructive worker'. It had nothing to do with construction; it was a phrase of Gandhi's, used to urge Indians to involve themselves in work at the grassroots, transforming people's lives. Political freedom from the colonizer was only supposed to be the first step—the First Freedom. Next came economic freedom, freedom from hunger and want—the Second Freedom, still a long way away for millions of Indians.

Lakshmi's father had served as the district president of the Congress Party in Delhi. His father had also edited a newspaper of the party, called the *Arjun*. Lakshmi had graduated with a BA during the peak of the freedom movement when students were a great force within it. He had been elected as the secretary of his college union, the Hindu College in Delhi University. He was a fiery speaker and led the students' marches during the Quit India movement. Born in 1925, he was just at the right age—about twenty years old—at the peak of the movement.

As the general secretary and director of the ICU, he was a gentle but firm boss. Every Saturday, all the 'volunteers', as we were called, even though most of us were salaried employees, met with Lakshmi. Each one of us had to report what we were doing, what were our thoughts. He would interrogate us and most of the time enable us to put our work into broader frames. For example, one of my colleagues was given the assignment of looking at a novel experiment, namely, the Delhi Milk Scheme (DMS). After returning from the gramdan villages, I was tasked with writing a report making a comparative analysis of the four or five state-sponsored rural development projects: Area development, Khadi and Village Industries Commission (KVIC), Community Development (CD), National Extension Scheme (NES) and Gramdan Development.

To my eyes, Lakshmi looked like a prince—I was reminded of Sir Galahad, the knight in the Arthurian romances we had grown up reading. I could visualise myself riding on a white horse with him into heaven or eternity. He was 'my man', even though he belonged to an inconvenient caste, that is to say, inconvenient from my point of view. Traders and businessmen, people of his caste were not scholars or professionals like us, and I knew immediately that this would cause problems with my family.

But there was a more pressing problem: in 1957, he got engaged to a young woman from a prominent family. The wedding was imminent, and I spent several days in agony at the thought that my own reticence had denied me my chance of happiness with the man I loved.

A diary entry from those years expresses my feelings more precisely than any retrospective account can:

Sunday, February 23

This day has been torture. If God made the engagement happen so that I might wake up, now that I have woken up he should help me. I have no scruples left and now pray that the engagement may be broken. I feel this is IT—nothing as heartbreaking as coming to this realization.

My 'catch' had slipped away from my hand, it seemed. But I would not be deterred. I decided I had to move. The attraction was too strong, the desire too compelling for me to bear it all in silence.

I plotted to be with him on our way to a wedding, the wedding of Manohar Benegal, the nephew of Lakshmi's friend, theatre director Som Benegal. All the ICU folk would be there. I knew that my 'Sir Galahad' would go to the house of Thomas Keehn, to see if he could get a ride to the wedding. Keehn had started an organization that worked with village craftspeople, with support from the Rockefeller Foundation, and was a friend of Lakshmi's. I got there a little earlier. Fortunately for me, the Keehns had already left. So I suggested we take a taxi together to the wedding.

As we settled in and the taxi started to move, I blurted out: 'I love you.' He looked at me with disbelief and a little anxiety: what was this woman saying? Had she lost her mind? He said nothing, and the taxi—a yellow-and-black cab of the kind common in Delhi in those times—made its rickety way towards the wedding.

'Are you listening?' I repeated. 'I love you. You have to marry me.'

Still he was silent. Then he spoke. 'You know I'm engaged.'

'Yes, I do! But you must break it. Because I love you.'

I launched into a speech of reproach. 'How could you? How could you get engaged without telling me?'

He was surprised. 'I didn't—I didn't know you cared for me.'

Our destination had arrived. We stepped out of the taxi and into the wedding marquee where we both got lost in the crowds. A little while later, he found me again and asked me to step out of the marquee. He had borrowed a station wagon from a colleague of his who was at the wedding and indicated that I should get into it. All this was done in complete silence, a silence that was one of his defining characteristics and one that never ceased to irk me. 'You are a sphinx! Talk to me,' I would often plead during our life together. 'I am no good at talking,' he would say. 'Just tell me what you want and I'll do it.' This would only make things worse. I would lose my temper and berate him for his silences, which I sometimes saw as an abdication of responsibility. But this was what he was: a man of action and few words.

He drove the station wagon to one of the quiet avenues in Delhi's Diplomatic Enclave where several countries had their embassies. The high walls and the patrolling security guards meant the streets were quiet and protected. We drove through those darkening, broad roads, past embassy after embassy, all in silence. I did not know what to say to break the silence. So I reached out and held his left hand. His response was electric. He pulled over the station wagon and parked in a dark spot on an inner avenue. He put his arms around me and kissed me, all the while saying nothing.

The passion and longing, suppressed for months, all came out over the next couple of hours. We held each other close, murmuring endearments, still not daring to talk about how things had come to this, or what we were to do next. Suddenly it was 2 a.m. 'Why didn't you reveal your love for me?' he asked. 'Well,' I replied, somewhat immodestly, 'I was surprised you were interested in anyone other than me.'

He didn't know what to do about his engagement. He went to see his fiancée's parents to apologize. They were utterly shocked. But they were deeply cultured people. Not a single word of reproach was uttered. The only thing her mother said to Lakshmi was, 'Jo Ishwar ki icchha,' (whatever God wills). Later that evening he went to apologize to his fiancée who was naturally very angry and hurt. But we both knew that we had found our life's partner in each other and any other commitment would be untruthful.

Lakshmi waited for me with the patience of a saint. I did not make it easy for him. Selfishly, I kept moving to faraway places. For the second time in my life, I went to Oxford, first for a job, then to do a degree. This kept me away from Delhi—the place where we had met and fallen in love—for four years.

❁

After my second stint in Oxford, I returned to my parents' home in Bangalore. I had maintained a regular correspondence with Lakshmi the whole time, and the new challenge was to find a way of being with him again in Delhi. I can remember being thoroughly baffled when he sent me a compass in the post. I wrote asking him to explain. Look at where it's pointing, he replied. North! I had to find a way to go north again.

I applied for and got a position as a lecturer in economics at Miranda House, a women's college in Delhi University. I moved to Delhi again and stayed with Sreedhar, then working as an engineer for the steel engineering firm, Dastur and Co. Lakshmi and I began to meet again, falling into an exciting new regime. On the days when we were to meet, I would step out of my brother's house on Rajdoot Marg in Chanakyapuri as if on the way to catch the bus to college. But after establishing that no one was watching me, I would go instead to Sardar Patel Marg where Lakshmi would pick me up and drive me to college in his car, an Ambassador. If—as often happened—I feared being spotted by someone who knew my brother, I would simply duck and hope for the best.

This went on for a while, and I thought I'd eventually muster up the courage to tell my parents about the situation and my intentions. But it took a while for me to do this. Every year during the university's summer vacation, I would return to Bangalore fully intending to tell them everything. But each time, I'd lose my nerve and have to tell Lakshmi that yet again, I had failed to do it. Then things came to a head after Lakshmi suffered a bereavement. His political mentor, Srinivas Malliah, died in 1965 and his body was flown down to Mangalore, his constituency, for the cremation. Lakshmi accompanied the body on the flight from Delhi, but after the funeral, he decided to carry on to Bangalore, to meet me.

Lakshmi was at his most vulnerable. Overwhelmed with grief, he gave me what amounted to an ultimatum. I had to marry him at once, or he would take the next train to the Gandhian ashram at Sevagram and dedicate himself to it entirely, never to return. I could not let this happen, but nor was I yet in a position to tell my parents.

So I told him to go and meet my father and broach the subject to see how it was received. If my father, unlikely as that seemed, agreed, then all was well and we could be married publicly and with my family's blessing. If, as was likelier, he denied us his blessing, then I would marry him anyway, but in secret, to assure him of my commitment to him. Then I could slowly work on preparing my family for the public announcement.

I learnt afterwards that Lakshmi's meeting with my father was an unmitigated disaster. My father had met Lakshmi once before in Bangalore, but I had introduced him as a former colleague at the ICU. It must then have come as a surprise to my father to find Lakshmi phoning him at the Taj Hotel in Bombay, where he was staying on a work-related trip. After some small talk, Lakshmi got to the point. He wanted to marry me and sought my parents' blessing. My father was livid. He told Lakshmi that marriage was out of the question, that he had best abandon any hope of such a thing, and that he was not interested in prolonging the conversation. Lakshmi had no choice but to leave, more than little embarrassed, but with a clear sense of what we now had to do.

Lakshmi told me that we would return to Delhi together, as I also had to get back to my job at Miranda House. There used to be a Janata Express from Madras, so we met at the railway station there. He had booked seats for us next to each other in what was called the chair car. The seats were cushioned chairs, which could be tilted back. The journey from Madras to Delhi was two nights and one and a half days. We kissed and held each other close all the way. For Lakshmi, it seemed to be the way he sought relief from his grief and chagrin.

When we reached Delhi, he took me to his apartment, 43 Golf Links, a residential colony in one of the most exclusive parts of the city. The house belonged to Dr Soni, an eminent dentist, whose sister, Dr Shanti Ghosh, was part of the refugee rehabilitation effort taking place under the auspices of the ICU. Lakshmi was part of the team, so she had persuaded her brother to let him and another volunteer, stay in the flat as it was empty—free of cost!

What started in the train could not be stopped. There for the first time we made love. This was 1965, and we got officially married only in 1966. I had to have two abortions, obviously secretly, in the course of the year. We just could not contain our passion.

We got married in secret on May 6, 1966. It had to be so, as my younger sister's marriage would have been jeopardized if it was known that a member of the family had married outside the caste. I could announce it only after she was safely married, which fortunately had been arranged for later that year.

After I was done with my lectures for the day, I took a bus from Miranda House to the Maidens Hotel, near the lieutenant governor's house in Old Delhi. Lakshmi had driven down in his white Ambassador car, carrying a diamond ring made by a friend of his who had given it to him free of cost. I got into the front seat, where he slipped the ring on my finger. Tingling with excitement, we drove to the Registrar's Office where we met three of his friends who had agreed to be witnesses at the wedding—though sworn to secrecy. After the documents had all been signed and we were husband and wife in the eyes of the law, the five of us drove together to the Imperial Hotel on Janpath where we had a coffee each. The bill came to fifteen rupees, and we had paid another fifteen at the Registry. The whole wedding had cost us a total of thirty rupees.

The next time I was in Bangalore with my family, I told my father what I had done. Over the previous two years I had broached the subject of my interest in marrying Lakshmi. But it was unacceptable. Members of the family reacted in different ways. My father showed no emotion at the revelation, just told me that I was dead to him—to put it as he said it, 'I have cremated you.' Sarathy, the most enlightened of my brothers, took me for a ride in his large car, and said, 'Jump out of the vehicle; we will say it was an accident.' The sense of shame at my marrying outside our caste was so deep.

My mother pointed to the pawn shops that we passed, on the way to meeting my married elder sister. All of them were run by Jains. With great agony in her voice, she pointed to their signboards and said, 'You will be with these kind of people.' But before I left Bangalore, quietly, and without telling my father, she took me out and bought me a sari. She also gifted me a little silver figurine of the god Krishna to guard me.

On July 15, 1966, I walked out of my father's house in Bangalore over his objections to my marriage to Lakshmi. Our house was a long way from the centre of Bangalore and the airport. There were no buses to take me to the airport. I could hardly expect to be escorted to what was effectively my elopement, in the family car. Lakshmi had arranged for a friend to meet me at the gate of the house and drive me to the airport, and put me on a flight back to Delhi. As I walked to the gate, I saw my mother's face in the window of her bedroom on the second floor. There was love in her face, and much anxiety, but no tears.

I arrived at 5 p.m. at the Delhi airport, where Lakshmi was waiting for me. Together we went to witness the opening of the Super Bazaar—the first retail cooperative store that was his brainchild—but from afar. As its principal organizer he was supposed to be there to receive Indira Gandhi, the prime minister, as she inaugurated the store, but since he had been at the airport to receive me when she arrived, we just watched the excitement from a distance!

Lakshmi was overwhelmed by my act of defiance, walking out with just a small duffel bag, no change of clothes and no money, to join him. 'She gave herself to me,' he liked to say to his friends, unlike the tradition which required me to be ceremonially given away by my father (the kanyadaan: literally, the virgin donated). 'She trusted me, leaving behind everything that meant security.' This gesture of mine and his memory of it was central to our relationship. He felt it placed him under an obligation, no matter how often I assured him it was I who had a debt to pay.

❁

The day after I returned from Bangalore, leaving behind my parental home, Lakshmi told me he had invited Kamaladevi Chattopadhyay for dinner. She arrived, portraying no particular surprise over my presence—she must have known who I was already. We were introduced; she smiled at me and gave me a sari. That was all—but we never looked back after that. The question of why I loved her instantly is one I am never able to answer to my satisfaction. Had I known of the radical spirit that animated her unlikely body, I might have been overwhelmed. Instead of an ideological similarity, though, a cultural similarity may have drawn us together.

Kamaladevi Chattopadhyay was a national icon long before I met her—a leader of India's freedom movement, a spirited activist and a sophisticated political thinker, an artiste and a patron of the arts, doyenne of the crafts movements, and one of the most important figures in moulding our new country's approach to culture. Lakshmi had worked with her for many years, having made common cause at the moment of India's Independence, when they both worked in refugee rehabilitation following Partition.

She was also fundamental to the women's movement that grew alongside the nationalist parties' struggle for Independence. She was part of an extraordinary generation who envisioned women as equal participants in the struggle to free India and Indian society, put themselves at the forefront of the fight, went to prison for their beliefs, and worked tirelessly to spread their message.

In 1988, she asked me to meet her in Mumbai (as Bombay was now called) and accompany her to Pune on a very special visit. The All India Women's Conference (AIWC), the institution set up by her friend, Margaret Cousins, was celebrating its golden jubilee, and she was, of course, to be chief guest—the most perfect candidate for the job. We travelled together to Pune; at the function, she wore a sari I had brought her as a gift. The AIWC received her with due pomp at the venue, and tried to escort her to the dais in the front of the hall where the celebration was being held. The chief minister of Maharashtra was waiting on the dais. Kamaladevi took a seat in the last row of the hall, and said she preferred not to take a seat on a raised platform, which connoted hierarchy and distance. The organizers nervously brought the ceremonial lamp, and all its accompanying dignitaries, down from the stage. Kamaladevi lit the lamp from her place at the back of the hall. Her revolutionary spirit had led us all, once again.

❁

Lakshmi's family home was the home of a freedom fighter, steeped in the traditions of India's struggle against British rule. His father, Sri Phool Chand Jain, born into a mercantile family that traded in jewellery and real estate, had been inspired to join this movement entirely of his own accord. He dropped out of school and went underground, organizing, writing and protesting. He would become a significant leader of the movement in Delhi, and this attracted the attention of the British authorities who jailed him for a time in the dungeons of Delhi's Red Fort.

Entering his home for the first time was unexpectedly traumatic for me. It was like nothing I had seen before. A typical old-fashioned haveli, the door leading into a courtyard, open to the sky but with three storeys of rooms on all four sides. The women of the household were all crowded in a kitchen on the right, saris drawn over their heads, faces almost completely covered, while the patriarch—my father-in-law—sat at a traditional desk in a room on the left, writing something. This was culturally alien to me, and I found it frightening to be among them—out of what fear, I'm no longer sure. My attitude to them was unforgivable, but it says something of the difference between the cultures of the south Indian family I had grown up in and that of Lakshmi's family, with its roots in Delhi and Rajasthan.

My sense of the otherness of Lakshmi's family was, in

the early stages of our marriage, so strong that I hesitated to accept his mother's kind invitations to lunch. When I was prevailed upon to accept, I insisted that I stay by Lakshmi's side throughout. When my first child, Gopal, was born and his family came to see us in the hospital, I insisted that they look at him only through the glass door of the nursery, refusing them permission to hold the baby.

I discovered in time that Lakshmi's parents and siblings were open-minded, interesting people, capable of enormous affection. Their way of life, once I got past the superficial appearances, was less traditional than I had at first supposed it to be. My father-in-law was no detached patriarch. He would pick up the vegetables in the market and chop them for his wife to cook. My mother-in-law—Chameli Devi—was no shy housewife. Raised in a deeply conservative Jain family where the women covered their faces almost completely, she threw all that off to join Gandhi's movement against British-made cloth. She was arrested when picketing the textile shops and taken to a jail in Delhi. A day later, she was taken further away to Lahore. My father-in-law had followed her there, fearing for her safety, and offered to pay the fine and have her released. But she would have none of it and rebuked him for his weakness, urging him to return home and be strong.

The more I came to learn about them, the more I came to feel like one of them.

As my own family became reconciled to my marriage, my husband and my lifestyle, they too, came to see his family as I saw them. They invited them to Bangalore, to our home, and the sense of relief that Lakshmi and I felt was immeasurable.

Even though my mother and my mother-in-law shared no language—my mother spoke no Hindi and my mother-in-law spoke no other language—they managed to express their mutual goodwill with smiles and gestures. My mother would utter a sentence or two of broken Hindi and my mother-in-law would smile and nod back.

Lakshmi's family taught me, more than any other Gandhian I have known, what it was to embody the Gandhian ethic in one's everyday life. In my years as a lecturer at Delhi University, I would often go to their house, which was near the university campus, and run up to my mother-in-law, asking her to sit down so that I could rest my head on her lap. Her lap seemed warming, and her hand stroking my head was the nearest to bliss that I have known.

CHAPTER NINE

The Turbulence of Wedded Life

To all outer appearances, Lakshmi was a quiet man, modest, introspective, soft-spoken and unaggressive. The passionate lover in him was well concealed. But it was the passion that was the glue that held us together all through our early years, enabling us to get through the struggles of our life together.

While our passion for each other had a strong element of common cause, there was an even more overwhelming presence of physical love, of romance. This longing and desire for each other had a cost in that it made us both vulnerable to pain and disillusionment.

My first disillusionment came the very next day of my moving into the flat at Golf Links after the formal marriage. It seemed to me as if I had climbed Mount Everest as at last, after eight years of secret romancing, we were under the same roof, living legitimately as man and wife.

But what was painful and led almost to a reversal of the passion was the fact that my husband had visitors from five-thirty in the morning. He had just opened India's first cooperative supermarket as part of a government effort to contain the private trade in consumer goods. This was a vast undertaking on his part, involving mobilizing grocers and suppliers of household goods, social activists and, of course, management colleagues. The shop opened at 9.30 a.m. and he needed to be in his office all day, as there would be a stream of visitors, managers, buyers waiting to catch him early, before he had even got there.

This sense of my husband as public property, obliged to pay attention to the clamouring of hundreds of other people, was a severe dampener on my passion. There was not to be the kind of romance I had expected, just the two of us by ourselves in our flat. I wanted to have a slow wake-up, cuddling and savouring the freedom of not hiding and pretending. Morning conversations over freshly brewed cups of coffee before we both went to work—but none of this happened.

After enduring a few months of this complete lack of romance, I complained so bitterly that he agreed to a kind of late honeymoon: a week in Kashmir. We would take our Ambassador car and drive to the Valley. This, too, was a disaster. He insisted on driving, even though I was an experienced driver—I had once driven a Land Rover along with other friends from London to Kabul. Worse, he was entirely silent during the drive. His silence set the tone for our holiday. He withdrew into himself and went very quiet, as he had a tendency to do in the face of conflict. Things only thawed in the evenings: our physical passion for each other was strong enough to overcome the ice that was forming over the rest of our relationship.

He had friends and admirers everywhere. He had hired a houseboat on a lake away from Srinagar. The owner was known to him—as were most of the artisans and entrepreneurs of the Kashmir Valley.

One afternoon, while we were docked into one of the banks of the lake, we looked across and there was Pandit Ravi Shankar with the Beatles, dressed in white kurta-pyjamas, like Ravi Shankar and my husband. I leapt up and pointed them out to Lakshmi, and almost cried saying I must meet them. Of course, as I found out later, Lakshmi knew most of the greats of that era—whether they were musicians or painters or theatre people. So, Ravi Shankar was an acquaintance! The people on the other bank then invited us, and I just had to tell the Beatles how crazy I was about their music and asked if I could take a photograph.

Soon I got pregnant and then began the other story of having an infant and not being able to do any of the things I wanted to, like going to work, or going out when I felt like. I felt trapped and resentful about the difference between my freedoms and his. When I look through my diaries from 1968, I find poem after poem of complaint, anger and bitterness, poems pronouncing that the ideal of an equal, companionate marriage is a hoax, doomed to devolve into the old stereotype: the man free, the woman in chains with the responsibility of childcare.

❁

The early relief and joy—the enchantment of finding one's lover, one's husband, the joy of having a child—soon descended into deep hostility. This is not a new story: thousands of women have felt it. But I felt, as my mother had feared, the costs of estrangement from my natal family. The normal practice in Indian households is for a woman to leave her husband's side for her delivery and go to her mother, who will help with the childbirth and then with the care of the baby for the first two or three months. Both my sisters have had this privilege, and so would millions of other women.

But in my case, Lakshmi and I had been excommunicated from the family. We decided not to move in with Lakshmi's family, warm-hearted though they were. We would go it alone. On the recommendation of some friends, we registered with a hospital in Delhi where most of the patients were expatriates. The baby was born on August 17, 1967. It was a boy, and we named him Gopal. When we brought the baby home, it was just me, my husband, and a part-time male cook, Sohan Singh, in the house. A little later, a maternal aunt of mine, who retained a soft spot for me despite my transgressions, came to stay. But it wasn't enough. Doing it almost entirely alone brought us to the brink of disaster. The infant came close to death after contracting a serious nursery infection but miraculously recovered. The constant sense of panic and crisis of those early months left us with a neurosis which lasted until our second child was three.

Even with the first child, I soon discovered that my freedom to move out of the house was restricted. Not only because childcare demanded attention, even though we had a new helper to look after the child, but also because the paranoia that I suffered from was really, looking back, insane. I was an overanxious mother and this affected me as well as Lakshmi. Since childbirth did not diminish our physical desire for each other, very soon I conceived again, but this pregnancy ended in a miscarriage.

Some of my family's hostility melted with the birth of our second child, actually our third. Sreenivasan was born on November 21, 1969. However, having two infants, whether one was one year old and the other three or whether one was three years old and the other five, just completely overwhelmed me with what can be called the 'women's condition'. Part of the trouble was my own overanxiousness about the children, and part was the fact that I had been used to a free life, with many interests and commitments. Now I found myself married to a public figure, equally bound to his projects—building the institutions of free India—who could not be expected to be homebound.

He was always willing to share the burdens, to change his plans when I asked. But it never felt enough. My neuroses grew, and I was constantly contemplating suicide. These thoughts came to me in sometimes frighteningly vivid fantasies: one day, when the children were at school and my husband at work, I would walk out of the flat and stand in the middle of the busy main road, waiting for a bus to mow me down. A crowd would gather around my body, lying in an absurd posture, my sari and blouse torn and exposing the skin. What of my parents, my husband and children? The fantasy didn't go so far.

Another time, when I fell ill with pneumonia and was confined to my bed, I seriously considered killing myself by not eating or drinking. I wrote poetry during these years, but most of it was never shown to anyone. Much of it concerned men and women and the impossibility of reconciling their interests. An extract from a poem, 'A Woman's Question', from the early years of my marriage, captures something of what I was feeling at the time:

You want me to be nature
endless, warm, forever ready
for you to rest your head, when weary—
to turn to when pushed by the mad world
But can I have an endless warm forever ready
place to rest when weary, or turn to when pushed?

Is it out of bounds to make these demands?
Am I stepping out of our comfortable
bounds in asking these questions?
Is this the emancipation that my sisters want?

'What I need,' I once said to Lakshmi, 'is a wife.'

'I see that,' he said. 'Can I be your wife?'

'Don't be silly,' I said. 'That would double my work—to keep house for you and then to teach you to be my wife?'

That was the flippant answer. In a flash, a bitterer answer came out: 'I'm sick of these responses from you. I know you mean them. I know you want my life to be light and happy, to support me in my interests and activities. But actually, your devotion to me, almost subservience, irritates me. It's unrealistic. It makes me feel like I'm dominating you, not appreciative enough of your work and your responsibilities.'

He looked injured. How could he not be? He was trying so hard. But I was lost. And I wasn't only being flippant. So much of our society, so many of our institutions seem to me to rest on the assumption of a wife working quietly away in the background, anticipating the needs of others and fulfilling them without resentment. No doubt this ought not to be so, but many things about the world need to be changed so that those of us without wives—or someone to play the traditional function of a wife—can lead the lives that wives make possible. Perhaps, I'd wonder in my idle moments, I could have two husbands. There is, after all, some precedent in the ancient Indian epics. There's a certain appeal in the idea of the public husband, the impressive man of public achievement, and the other a modest householder. But no, I eventually decided. It's a silly fantasy. I couldn't see myself managing a sane sex life with two men.

❁

Our economic situation in the early years of our marriage had been precarious. Lakshmi was earning an honorarium of Rs 500 a month as a member secretary of the handicrafts board, a position which also gave him access to a car and a driver. I was then on a lecturer's salary which came to Rs 501. With two young sons to care for, this didn't leave us with much money for luxuries or activities outside the home like shopping and eating out.

By 1972, however, Lakshmi's friends had helped him to find the economic security he had so long lacked. These were friends who had known him as part of the students' movement in the years of the freedom struggle. Two of them were now businessmen and they helped Lakshmi set up a consultancy service, focusing on small-scale industries and similar areas where he had some expertise and experience.

By this time, I had resigned from my lectureship at Miranda House and taken up a fellowship in the Centre for Advanced Studies at the Delhi School of Economics. I was working on a paper on the partition of the Indus River—the allocation of water between India and Pakistan being a prominent political issue at the time. We moved into a flat in Jorbagh, and the children were now both in school. Life began again.

The Indian Council for Social Science Research (ICSSR) helped me to set up a new field-based project on the unrecognized contribution of women to the economy. The dining room and spare room in our flat became the 'office'; I employed two research assistants and a stenographer. I started to travel abroad, starting with the first UN World Conference in Mexico in 1975, from which I ended up having to rush back after Prime Minister Indira Gandhi declared a state of Emergency, and there was briefly a threat that the borders would be closed. Lakshmi took care of the children while I was away, without complaint. I was busy and intellectually occupied with things I found interesting and important; I was happy. Lakshmi would say to me, 'Fly!'

CHAPTER TEN

The Delhi Circle

Our home soon turned into a semi-public space, a hub for friends, colleagues and public figures to gather and talk and debate at length. During and after the Emergency, our house was the site of innumerable discussions of politics and economics, particularly among critics of the Congress Party of that period. We were seen as intellectual and political equals and comrades, rather than the conventional husband and wife pair.

Invitations would arrive in the post addressed to both of us, asking us to address a rally together, or to join political struggles, or visit a project in the field. We attracted the attention of intellectuals, political leaders, journalists, both from India and from abroad. Economists and other social scientists would visit, and sometimes American feminists curious to learn about the work I was beginning to do in the Indian women's movement.

Then began the high point of our life together. Our personal relationship flourished in these years, our public and private lives coming together, our public and private passions complementing each other. The envies, jealousies, frictions and resentments of the early years began to dissolve.

❁

Lakshmi was among the most versatile personalities in Delhi in the 1960s and 70s. He encompassed the intellectual space, the public policy space as well as the institutional space. He would be on the governing council or the advisory board of ten institutions at one time. He was part of the birthing of new ideas in Delhi. He was recruited to be on the planning board of Uttar Pradesh, on the one side, and Tamil Nadu, on the other.

If Verghese Kurien, founder of the famous Anand Milk Union Limited (AMUL) enterprise, wanted to set up a group to review what was happening in the White Revolution and the cooperative movement, Lakshmi would be there. If C. Subramaniam wanted to re-examine the trade policy as the minister of commerce, Lakshmi would be part of the group. If the government wanted to set up a promotion of the Northeast, not only was Lakshmi there, he even founded a collective which brought all Northeastern states together, to form an outlet called the 'Seven Sisters' to sell products made in the Northeast. The Seven Sisters shops were opened in many cities apart from New Delhi.

In 1974, when a terrible drought in Bihar was followed by a students' uprising, Jayaprakash Narayan, or JP as he was known, requested Lakshmi to visit and see for himself the depth of the famine and think of responses. Both of us, Lakshmi and I, travelled to Patna and stayed with JP and his wife, Prabhavati Devi, in their house. We drove out to see the horror of parched fields and skeletal people. As it has been recorded, this was the beginning of the uprisings that led to the imposition of the Emergency by Indira Gandhi in 1975, suspending political freedoms in India.

In the interim, many groups came together to formulate economic policies and programmes that needed to be put on the ground in India, at least in Bihar. JP invited me to join these informal councils in Patna and to record the conversations. People who sat around the table came from diverse political backgrounds—there were the socialist leaders, Ram Manohar Lohia and Madhu Limaye, and the leader of the Jan Sangh, Atal Bihari Vajpayee, who later became India's prime minister.

Lohia would insist on talking in Hindi. Once, I summoned the courage to object. Lohia was furious but the group took it in good humour. He eventually thawed and spoke a few words in English. I recall these meetings as an opportunity to come face to face with some of the senior political leaders of those times and to hear how they envisioned building an economically just India.

Later I had to convene similar consultations in Delhi when JP was trying to formulate an economic programme for post-Emergency India. Even economists like Mrinal Dutta Chaudhuri and Pranab Bardhan, who were not in thrall of JP, felt deeply curious about him, and came over to our house in Jorbagh, first to meet him over dinner, and later to sit with me to draw up a paper.

Alas, those handwritten papers—there was no computer at that time, everything was written by hand or on the typewriter—were thrown into the Yamuna by my father-in-law after the Emergency was declared. He feared that if they were discovered by the police, they could lead to my arrest. The remembrance of the loss still bothers me.

PART FOUR

Touch

'Sex pleasure in woman is a kind of magic spell; it demands complete abandon; if words or movements oppose the magic of caresses, the spell is broken.'

—Simone de Beauvoir

CHAPTER ELEVEN

Hidden Dangers, Secret Pleasures

My experience with touch revealed that Simone de Beauvoir's generalization is misplaced or does not work out many times. There is the good, the bad and the evil.

The year was 1943. It was the middle of the Second World War, and India was involved with the Allied war effort as an important source of supplies. I was ten years old at the time. My father was posted in Madras as the controller of civil supplies, seconded from the Mysore government. We lived in a house on the beach. In October 1943, a lone Japanese reconnaissance exploded a bomb on the coast of Madras, and the family had to be evacuated to somewhere safer.

It was one of those evenings when my mother and aunt had gone out to the ladies' club, and my uncle—my mother's brother—was the only grown-up in the house. He asked me into one of the bedrooms, where he was sitting with a book.

'What are you reading?' I asked him.

'This is a medical textbook,' he said. 'It teaches you about all the parts of the human body. I need to study it for my exams.'

He proceeded to show me the illustrations in the textbook. One page had the picture of a male body that showed the male sexual organ. 'Come,' he told me, 'I'll show you what this is.'

The room had barred windows but these were located fairly high on the wall so that passers-by on the street couldn't see anything if they looked in. There were no curtains, which were a rarity in those days.

'You can see the road from my room, you know that?' he said.

To show me the road, he picked me up. I held the bars while he held me from the back. Then he turned me around and asked me to hold on to his neck so that he could swing me. It was a nice game, I thought at first, as he swung me away from him, then back into his body. Then he held me close and asked me to open my mouth. When I did, he put his tongue into it.

'This is a cow-and-calf game,' he said. 'Suck my tongue like the calf sucks the cow's udders.' I did as he asked, then decided I didn't like it and asked to be put down.

'There's another cow-and-calf game,' he said, and asked me to kneel and be the calf. Then he pulled out his penis and asked me to suck it as I had his tongue. I found the experience very odd and ran away, not then concerned about the 'game', and thought little of it at first.

When my mother and aunt returned from the club, I told them about my day. I said my uncle had shown me pictures, and had tried to put something funny in my mouth. They were shocked and very scared. They immediately took me aside and said I was to tell no one, certainly not my father. Nor was I ever to go into my uncle's room again. From that day on, they never once left me alone in the house when my uncle was there. That was all they did.

I see it now from their point of view. He was the only son of my maternal grandmother. He had been married and had four children. He had just lost his wife, who had died of burns, and was entirely dependent on my parents for shelter and support while he studied for his medical degree. If my father got to know of it, he could have been put in prison, thrown out of the house at the very least. So the women, his sisters and mother, protected him.

One of the most persistent anxieties that mothers must face is for their daughters and what might happen to them while they are away. It is now a well-established fact that working women who must leave their daughters alone in the house with grandfathers or uncles are aware that those daughters are vulnerable to rape by these close family members. It is not by strangers that women are most threatened.

It is possible that they confronted my uncle about the matter, but if they did, I never knew of it. He continued to live with us. The only change was that I was supervised much more closely by my mother and aunt. As the years went by and the family moved from Mysore to Bangalore, this uncle would often visit us. At first, my aunt would lock me away in a room while he was there. As I grew older and this was no longer possible, I tried my best to stay away when he was around. I found later that I was far from being his only victim. He had also molested a cousin of mine to whom I was very close.

When I did find myself in the same room as him, he gave me the look that rapists are supposed to give their victims, a look that suggests intimacy. Once, he even appeared at my front door after I was married. The sight of him brought such panic and fear that I simply shut the door on his face.

When he died, I flatly refused to attend the funeral. My sisters and other relatives tried to put pressure on me to go, saying it would look bad to the extended family if I wasn't present at the funeral of our mother's only brother. I was forced to tell them why I would not, could not, go. Their reaction was unsympathetic, and I now know, all too common. 'I wonder why he went for you? You always were a flirt. You must have invited it.'

❁

But growing up, I also discovered touch was not always bad.

In the large house in which we lived in another city years after this experience, there were two bathrooms, one for my father and one for my mother. It was a luxury but the owner was following the requirements of an American man who lived there earlier.

I had a sense of pleasure when I touched my breasts. I must have been eleven years old and two little lumps had appeared on my chest. I found that touching them gave me a tingling sensation. So in order to make it more exciting, I developed an idea. There were some kittens in the house, to whom we would try and feed milk through a pippet—a short glass tube with a rubber ball, which we used to use to fill our fountain pens with ink.

When my parents were out and I was back from school, I would pick up one of the kittens and enter my father's bathroom through the back door. I would bring some milk from the kitchen, and opening my blouse, would spread the milk on my nipples and put the kitten's mouth there. The kitten, with its slightly rough tongue, would lick the nipples and I would feel sensations of unimaginable pleasure. I would go on dripping milk on to my breasts and the kitten would lick. All of a sudden the kitten would stop licking and I would wipe myself with water from the tap. I would leave the bathroom quietly through the back door and put the kitten back with his mother. It was so pleasurable that even now when I think about it, I can feel the pleasure. Why did I do it? What was this compulsion of feeling the excitement of touch on the body?

CHAPTER TWELVE

Breaking Codes

My first romantic encounter with a man happened when I was twenty.

It was 1953. I had just graduated in Bangalore, and was literally doing nothing at home. Sreedhar had told me about the students' seminar, which I have mentioned earlier, convened in Bangalore by the Quakers. I persuaded my parents to let me go for a while. While the other students were all living in the camp, I went from home in a car with a driver, who was stationed there to 'protect' me while I joined the group, for a limited period, namely half a day, on each of the days that the seminar was on.

The seminar introduced me to Gandhi's ideas which determined much of the journey of my life. But I also found myself drawn to David Hoggett, one of the two young men who had come from Gandhi's ashram in Wardha.

David would play the flute. He had stayed for a while at the Visva-Bharati University in Santiniketan as a volunteer and had learnt Rabindra Sangeet. He would sing it in Bengali with a slight British accent. Then he would play the same song on the flute. It was fascinating. Then he would suddenly break out into English folk songs and play that also on the flute. He came from a family of art and music. His brother was a painter. David had joined what was called in those days the Service Civil International and landed in India.

I always loved to sing and dance, so I learnt the geets from him, then as I learnt them properly, I accompanied him, while he played the recorder: 'Tomaro Ashime Praano Mono Loye', 'Pagla Hawar Badol Dine', 'Klanti Amar Khoma Koro'. As we engaged in this dueting, we found ourselves becoming attracted to each other. David held my hand, and I found it very exciting.

While the seminar was getting over, around 5 p.m., we disappeared behind some hedges, and I experienced my first kiss, on the lips. It was so seductive, one did not want to stop. We would have this kissing session every evening till the seminar came to an end, and then David proposed to me and asked me to run away from home. He and his comrade from Sarva Seva Sangh Ashram plotted how I would do that. They would post me a khadi sari and blouse, and a rail ticket to Wardha. I would then wear the sari and find my way to the station and run away. They did post the sari (I still have it, a white sari with a purple border) but I chickened out, much to their disappointment. They showed no anger, though.

While this friendship lasted and influenced me for the rest of my life, it also broke the physical barrier that we are made to feel when we engage with the other sex in physical relationships.

Later when I arrived in England, during that one year when I was in Ruskin College, David was my constant companion. He had a motorbike and we would drive off on weekends to London to dance at the folk dance school or to the north to join a folk dance festival. On some of these trips, I even slept with him in the same sleeping bag. We kissed and petted but neither did he make a move to have intercourse nor did I know what that was all about. The sensations seemed to begin with the mouth and end with the breasts. At that time I did not actually know what was the sexual act of penetration and the organs related to it, and men seemed to have guessed or sensed that about me and never went beyond.

❁

The Quaker connection took me to another seminar of young people that took place in Saarbrücken in Germany, as I have mentioned earlier in these memoirs. I don't quite know how I did it, where I got the money for the travel, the visas, and most of all, the guts to travel on my own across continents. But I did it.

The camp was a wonderful experience where I met young people from many countries—a girl from Jamaica who sang and danced to calypso music, and taught me the dance; a Norwegian girl who later became a famous professor of anthropology, Astrid Nypan; a Yugoslav youth, Vojin Dmitrivic, who later became a famous journalist. The young people at the camp broke up into twos in the evenings, pairing girls and boys, and wandered off into the woods for some loving. I paired with Vojin whom I fell in love with and had my second experience of kissing and petting—so intoxicating. Then, as I have mentioned earlier, another participant, a young Dane, Bjorn Thomsen, persuaded me to hitchhike with him, after the seminar, all through northern Europe and then to England.

Our first stop was Frankfurt. My father had friends in Germany and asked me to contact one of them, the head of AGFA, the film manufacturers. He took one look at the young Dane and me, and assumed we were lovers. He threatened he would tell my father, which he did. I learnt this from my mother much later. How worried she was when she heard I had got into a relationship in Europe.

The AGFA man, I remember his name was Wilde, took us out for dinner. It was the first good meal we had in several weeks. We stayed in youth camps; we wandered through Germany and went north to Scandinavian countries, swam in the sea and finally ended up in England. It took us all of three weeks.

In Oxford, one of the 'foreign' students, an Austrian, and I began to touch and kiss and this went on for the year. It seemed as if these liaisons were a natural experience for men and women living in proximity and I really was drawn into this kind of intimacy and physical experience.

In 1958, when I was in Harvard, I could not resist the physical approaches of a handsome young German novelist. Somehow his personality and his interest in me aroused an enormous amount of desire for the two months that I was in Harvard. We would spend almost every evening hiding in various corners of the Harvard yard and behind buildings and so forth, hugging and kissing and petting. But not really engaging in sex; it always ended, to put it crudely, above the waist. In his case, he even took the plunge of proposing a trip to Staten Island and booking rooms in a hotel. But even though we were sleeping together, somehow, whether it was the man's understanding of my innocence, or something I unconsciously conveyed, there was no attempt to go further than 'above the waist'.

This is to show that these kinds of dalliances with men were very normal for young women in the West in those days. The interesting part is that because of my upbringing, I was unwilling to give up my virginity. It was like being in Rome and doing what the Romans did—and sticking to Indian traditions as well!

❀

The second period in Oxford (1959–62) had other temptations. One of the young men I attracted came from the early Oxbridge group in Delhi, a group that I had got involved with when I came back from Ruskin College in 1956–57, that is, when I met Amartya Sen for the first time. But this young man, who I met again in Oxford, courted me and really wanted to go beyond courting to marriage. Regrettably for him, I felt no attraction for him. I was attracted to another young Indian man who was doing his postgraduation, and spent most of my evenings with him.

This kind of unspoken rule of keeping away from actual sexual engagement seemed to be quite normal amongst Indian girls at Oxford at this time. I say this because while I was there, there were other Indian girls or women who were also engaged in romantic encounters with young men but mostly of the kind that stopped at a level of petting and kissing and did not go beyond into deeper sexual engagement. It was a sort of invisible control that came from our backgrounds, our culture, the attitudes of our parents, the presence of those attitudes in our own lives, and the fact that we were so happy to have that limited experience of physical love.

❁

I had one unwelcome experience in Oxford in 1958 when I worked as a research assistant for an eminent Swedish economist. He was in Oxford, courtesy Balliol College, to work on his magnum opus, a three-volume work on development. He had senior colleagues to assist him and was looking for a junior research assistant from Asia.

I was twenty-five. I had grown up in south India, and lived in Bangalore. I had graduated from a women's college in Bangalore, with special papers in mathematics and economics, and was awarded three gold medals by the University of Mysore for topping the results in maths and in general totals. Later, in 1955, I had studied at Ruskin College in Oxford and got a diploma in the social sciences.

Another qualification which seemed relevant to his work was that earlier, in 1958, after attending the Harvard Summer Seminar with a grant from the Asia Foundation, I had travelled to almost every country in Asia, starting from Hawaii, to Japan, Vietnam, Cambodia, Hong Kong, Malaysia and Myanmar (erstwhile Burma).

The professor had mentioned to some of his friends in the subcontinent his interest in recruiting a young person from Asia to add to his assistance for writing this major book on the region and its economic prospects. One of these contacts knew me and suggested that I apply. I promptly applied, and was invited for an interview at the residence of the Swedish ambassador, Alva Myrdal's residence. I was thrilled when I was selected.

I travelled to Oxford to join the team. My job was to research, prepare notes and write a rough draft for the chapters on the political situation of the countries, a section called 'Political Background', which was to serve as a background for the other chapters focused on the economy. I found accommodation, a room in a boarding house set up by the same Russian orthodox group, whom I had known when I was at Ruskin College.

The professor would often host dinners for his team as well as some of his colleagues from the university, in the best restaurants in Oxford. One such evening, after a big dinner at a restaurant at Windsor Castle, an hour or more away from the city of Oxford, the professor offered to drop me at my lodgings. I accepted his offer without a qualm, since I had no indication that he was a predator. I sat in the seat next to him while he drove.

We were speeding along the main road, when he laughed and dug the fingers of his left hand into my crotch. I used to wear a sari in those days so it was not difficult for him to plunge his fingers between my thighs in one quick move. Stunned, I shouted, 'What are you doing? Take your fingers out.' His response was to laugh and say sardonically, 'You could not be a virgin, what are you trying to tell me?'

He kept pushing his fingers in, dragging me towards him with that left hand, and I was frightened to death. But I found the courage to put my hand on the door handle and say: 'I am going to open the door and jump out. Of course I will die but you will be prosecuted and go to jail.' As he heard the click of the door, he removed his hand. He abused me, alleging that I was pretending to be a virgin, that I must surely have had sex by now, and so what was this fuss all about. Then he drove me back to my lodgings and went his way home.

The trauma deepened the next day when I went to work. He was in his room, surrounded by our colleagues. Seeing me walk in, he started to laugh and said: 'This woman is an uncut diamond. She is not educated enough to work with me.' He then served notice on me, saying I was inadequate for the job and my salary would stop from that day.

There I was, in a foreign country, without the support of family, subject to the vengeful wrath of a sexual predator. I had no confidante to whom I could go for counsel, and knew of no institutional mechanism to seek redressal. No one spoke openly of these things, though it was obvious enough that most people knew what went on and sustained the toxic climate by their omissions even more than by active collusion. It was the late 1950s and this was just how things were.

It was a crushing blow, and it was hard not to let myself think that he was right: maybe, despite being top of my year in mathematics in Mysore, despite my diploma from Ruskin College, maybe I was, as my employer maliciously insinuated, not all that intelligent. I was a young woman and my intellectual self-confidence was, at the best of times, fragile; survivors of assault, I have since learnt, are often wracked by feelings of guilt and inadequacy, prone to self-blame for advances they did nothing to provoke. This intellectual humiliation was bad enough, but it got worse: I was told that my employer was withdrawing from his obligation to pay my return fare to India.

During the few months that I had worked with the professor, I had struck up a friendship with some others of his team. Apart from Ester and Mogens Boserup, the Danish academics, especially skilled in statistics, there was Paul Streeton, a brilliant scholar who was a Fellow of Balliol College.

Isolated and without resources, I went to Paul, who advised me to reach out to St Anne's, at that time known as the most progressive college, interested in wider issues, and ask to be admitted to their philosophy, politics and economics (PPE) course. I approached St Anne's to see if they would admit me for an Oxford degree. They did.

But the real blow came three years later when I sat for the final exam for the degree. I could not write answers. I found myself go blank. The assault and rejection by the professor had destroyed my self-worth. With great difficulty, the compassionate dons of Oxford allowed me to pass and get my degree, but it was not a good outcome. My teachers could not understand what had happened to a student they considered one of the best and expected to get what in Oxford is called a congratulatory first.

I realized that my self-confidence had been destroyed. My intellectual self had been affected by that traumatic dismissal. I had come to Oxford glowing with pride that I had been selected out of a whole number of nominees from South Asia. Later, I began to feel that I was not selected for my intellect but for my body.

Looking back, I can see the risks involved in feeling free. Currently the #MeToo movement reveals the risks that women take when working for men but the atmosphere is one where there can be retribution. But in those times, there was no such 'outside' support.

PART FIVE

The Academy

'We live in a fantasy world, a world of illusion. The great task in life is to find reality.'

—Iris Murdoch

CHAPTER THIRTEEN

Oxford Once More

St Anne's was a women's institution founded in the late nineteenth century that had recently become a full-fledged college of the university and was known to be run by empathetic women with liberal attitudes. A little desperate, a little sheepish, I knocked at the door of the economics tutor, Peter Ady, a friend of Paul Streeton's. Peter was, despite her name, a woman. Confident, self-assured, and mildly eccentric—she was dressed in riding breeches, a whip in her hand, and talking on the telephone when I entered her office.

I said nothing about the assault and to the best of my knowledge, she never knew of it. I only said I wanted to study economics and asked if there was any way in which St Anne's could admit me. Incredibly, she said yes (perhaps she had been briefed by Paul Streeton), but economics at Oxford was taught as part of a three-subject honours degree in philosophy, politics and economics, and she could only take me on if the St Anne's Fellows in the other two subjects agreed. If they were game, then we could go on the next problem: how was I to going to pay the college fees?

Soon after, I was standing nervously at the gate of

Jenifer Hart's house. Hart was the college Fellow in politics. Formidably clever, she had been a powerful and influential civil servant during the Second World War. She made no secret of her left-wing convictions, and had once been an active Communist; this fact would bedevil the second half of her life, when she spent years denying accusations that she had been a Soviet spy. She wasn't in the house when I arrived, and I stood leaning on her fence and fidgeting until she appeared on her bicycle. Like Peter, she did not ask me for any credentials; she only wanted to know how I intended to support myself.

I met Iris Murdoch last of all. The meeting took place in her tutorial office. She was a warm, beautiful woman, with a low, reflective voice. Her large blue eyes looked at you with a piercing intensity; sometimes I felt like she could see through me. Iris, too, agreed to admit me, and the three Fellows then sent me to the principal of St Anne's, Lady Mary Ogilvie. Lady Ogilvie was, as her title implied, a grande dame. Friendly, kind and shrewd, she was known for 'taking chances' on unconventional students, seeing promise in them even when no one else did. Her time as principal of St Anne's would prove to be one of the most eventful in its history as she turned the fledgling institution in her charge into an academically serious yet inviting college. Lady Ogilvie, to my infinite gratitude, was willing to take a chance on me. She and her vice-principal, Marjorie Reeves, also had good, practical advice about how I was to get the money together: I could write to several British trusts that gave small educational grants to students—the Spalding Trust, Cadbury Trust and so forth and my other expenses—food, 'digs'—could be covered by part-time work.

Immediately, I sent off several letters requesting to be considered for a grant. I was successful, but only partially. Money would come in dribs and drabs, often covering only a term at a time. My degree was done in a state of extreme uncertainty, it never being clear at the end of one term if I would have enough money to cover the fees for the next. It was harrowing, and when I could get past the constant anxiety, a little bit exhilarating too. Some of the common sense and the dislike for grumbling that I had learnt at Ruskin certainly came in handy now.

On the weekends and vacations, I washed dishes at the Cavendish Restaurant at the corner of Broad Street; this more or less paid for my food. I also worked part-time as a cleaner in the house where I was lodging for the year, which covered most of my other expenses. It was far from luxurious, but it got me through my degree.

Teaching at Oxford happened mostly in weekly tutorials, one or two students with a tutor in her study, discussing an essay we had spent the week writing. This could be an oddly powerful and intimate experience, so concentrated was the attention paid to one's writing and thoughts during the hour we had with our tutors.

The women were fascinated by the saris I wore. Peter once insisted on photographing me as I bicycled in a sari; she had been faintly incredulous that it could even be done. Iris, during her philosophy tutorials with me, would sometimes say, 'Sit further back, won't you, so that the sunlight falls on your face.' I did not find their attention intrusive; in fact, it was flattering, and never translated into any misbehaviour or harassment.

The quality of passionate intensity was especially marked with Iris. This was channelled, quite properly, into the philosophy she was teaching me, and I was never treated with anything other than the respect due to a student and fellow inquirer. Her affection and respect for me during those years would became the basis for a lifetime's friendship.

One incident particularly stands out in memory. Iris had set for my weekly essay some such topic as, 'Reason is, and ought only to be, the slave of the passions...' (Alexander Hume). Like her colleagues in Oxford at the time, Iris disliked high-flowing abstractions about 'reason' and 'passion'. She was slowly coming into her own as a novelist at the time, and she was attracted to the French novelist-philosophers of those years—Jean-Paul Sartre, Albert Camus and Gabriel Marcel. She was almost unique in Oxford in taking an interest in such figures; her colleagues, such as the moral philosopher R.M. Hare, were much more interested in logic and the close analysis of everyday language, words like 'ought'and 'right'. Iris, by contrast, was deeply interested in human psychology and the complexity of human motivations.

She asked me for an example that might make Hume's deliberatively provocative claim clearer and more vivid. I responded, ingenuously, with the first thing that came to mind: a man caught between his duty to his wife and his great passion for his mistress. Reason says one thing, desire another. But what power can reason have when it is up against the force of a man's deepest passions? And even if he ended up staying with his wife, as reason and duty demanded, wouldn't it be because he found that it was his passion for doing his duty that was the stronger force? Deep down, isn't it passion all the way?

Iris was sufficiently impressed by my essay to exercise her influence with the college to find me an 'exhibition'—Oxfordese for a small scholarship—that kept me going for a few more months. I can remember walking nervously into Lady Ogilvie's room to find her sitting at a desk with Iris, positively beaming at me: 'Miss Murdoch tells me you wrote a brilliant essay,' and asking me to explain it. At one point, when no grants were forthcoming from any of the trusts that had supported me in the past, Iris stepped in and paid my fees from her own funds.

Iris was a very open-minded teacher. She had none of her colleagues' triumphalist attitudes to Western civilization and its intellectual heritage. Again, almost uniquely among her philosopher colleagues, she was interested in Buddhism and in Gandhi, and drawn to Indian spiritual traditions for their emphasis on shedding the ego.

On one occasion, I can remember talking to her about Rousseau and his idea of the 'general will', the will of a community that lies deeper than the individual wills of the community's members and can be elicited by getting people to think beyond their own private interests or preferences. To her, the idea had seemed a historical artefact, but I pointed out that there was at that time a man in India who was walking the length and breadth of the country asking landlords and villages to donate land to the landless, to own their land collectively, appealing, in other words, to the general will. She did not dismiss the analogy as irrelevant, as a different tutor might have done, but asked me to tell her more, and said she would like some day to visit India and walk with him. She was always ready to learn about things of which she was ignorant, humility unexpected in a woman of her intellectual attainments.

She was fascinated by India, by Hinduism and Buddhism and their spiritual and philosophical traditions. Many years later, she realized her desire to come to India—as an invitee to one of Prime Minister Indira Gandhi's 'Round Tables' to which eminent intellectuals from across the world were invited. (Indira Gandhi had in fact been a friend of hers at school, and they kept up a correspondence for many years.) Once she was finished with her official engagements, she spent time with me walking in Lodhi Garden, coming to dinner at our house, and playing with Gopal, then aged one. I even took the opportunity to interview her on Indian national television. When she returned to Oxford, she sent us baby clothes and requested pictures of the little boy. The conversation we had started in tutorials lasted for many decades, all the way into her final devastating struggle with Alzheimer's disease, which deprived the world of a unique—I do not hesitate to use the word—genius.

Iris Murdoch, Peter Ady, Jenifer Hart: three supremely intellectual women, all taking me seriously as a fellow thinker. This kind of respectful intellectual engagement was much more help to me than any conventional therapy could have been. I was a woman among other women, and we were bound by ties of intellectual sympathy. I was being valued for my intelligence, hard work and achievement. I was a few years older than the other undergraduates at St Anne's, but they took me to their hearts and many remain close friends of mine all these years later. I bought a cheap bike and cycled everywhere: economy and responsibility were forced on me by my circumstances. But I managed to have a rich and active social life, going to parties when I could. My wounds were beginning to heal, but the process was slow and halting.

I had managed to make something of myself in Oxford after the inauspicious beginning of my second stint there. I had the support and encouragement of my teachers and peers, but the sense of humiliation never entirely left me. Unable to speak of my experience of assault to anyone, I felt a piercing loneliness even when I was—in other people's eyes—happy and carefree. I had recurring flashbacks of the episode. I frequently woke up from nightmares of it, and the feeling of self-doubt would filter into my waking hours. When I took my final exams—'Schools' as they are called in Oxford—some of this under-confidence filtered through. I struggled to get all my preparation onto the exam script, sometimes struggled to write anything at all, and did not get the First that my tutors had expected.

My two periods at Oxford were by no means easy. I was poor, often overworked, and in a state of constant anxiety. But I grew up there as I could not have done in more congenial circumstances. My own story cannot be generalized, but I hope it can give hope to others who have had to fend for themselves in an alien environment or deal with the after-effects of assault without the sympathy and support of others. It is possible—though it will always be difficult—to recover from assault and humiliation.

It will seem surprising today, given how easily people can keep in touch—by e-mail and phone and video-conferencing with their families even while studying abroad. But in those years, there were only letters and those took weeks to arrive. My family was aware of where I was and what I was doing, but there were so many children to keep track of that I do not think they spent too much time worrying about me. I was on my own, and felt no obligation to keep them constantly informed of my every move. I certainly did not tell them of my struggles. Freedom and self-reliance come with risk, and the life of a free woman cannot be insulated from hurt. Sometimes the most we can do is to learn not to be broken by our experiences, to rebuild our lives with what materials are at hand, bit by bit, slowly and patiently.

CHAPTER FOURTEEN

The Student Becomes a Teacher

In the long run, my exam results did not matter. I had made a good enough impression on my tutors at various Oxford colleges with my performance in tutorials for them to write me strong references. When I returned to India, I was able to find a job at Miranda House in Delhi University, as a lecturer in economics. Miranda House was, like St Anne's, a women's college, and was, in the 1960s, one of the liveliest institutions in Delhi. Much of this liveliness came from the academics who were teaching there.

Some of the women who were lecturers there, such as Roma Mitra, Kamla Achayya and Kanti Shastri, were women who were politically minded. Kanti taught in the economics department, Krishna Essaul in the English department and Roma in history. They were what one could call radical without being Marxists. Roma Mitra was a close friend of Ram Manohar Lohia, a leading socialist. There were suggestions that she was his partner. Krishna Essaul was clearly a leftist. She had married a Russian. Kanti Shastri was also a radical though perhaps not a Marxist. Students and teachers were all extremely alive politically and socially. They were all engaged with drama and debates, and some of the plays that Miranda House put forward, sometimes along with the neighbouring men's college, St Stephen's, were directed by Krishna. Roma Mitra, who lived in Lohia's house, would often invite her fellow teachers to the house, and they would discuss current affairs with him.

It wasn't only the teachers who were politically active, the students were equally impressive. Brinda Karat (at that time Brinda Das) was a first-year student in the English Honours course when I joined Miranda House. Politically and socially active, Brinda was a talented and charismatic actress to boot. I remember her as a live wire, the protagonist of every play she was cast in. She was briefly a student of mine in my 'Pass Class'—a class in economics for those students who were studying for Honours in a different subject. I believe she still remembers that class, though I certainly cannot accept any credit or blame for her political formation or subsequent commitment to both Marxism and feminism (my classes, to the best of my knowledge, involved discussions on neither subject). Miranda House, in the era that I was there was, in today's parlance, a 'happening' place and I often felt that it was more intellectually powerful, politically alive and had better students than the male colleges and other male spaces.

The greater part of this energy came mostly from the English and history departments. The economics department was full of women with onerous family duties—demanding husbands and small children—and they were always divided between these two parts of their lives. The college offered them some brief respite from domestic duties, but they were always being called back to attend to some problem or responsibility at home. I can see the extent of their difficulties now, having since experienced some of what they did myself, but at the time, I must confess I was much less understanding. Young and unmarried, I was rather put off by the sight of my departmental colleagues sitting in the staffroom, knitting and talking about babies. How much more exciting it was to walk down to the coffee shop at the Delhi School of Economics nearby and sit with Amartya Sen or Sukhamoy Chakraborty as their students (largely male) gathered around them, talking about ideas and politics. I enjoyed those settings and conversations much more than what confronted me in my own staffroom. My friend, the American feminist writer Gloria Steinem, once playfully told me I was a bit of a 'queen bee' in that milieu. I greatly enjoyed being the only, or one of the few, women in a room of authoritative intellectual men, holding my own in conversation with them. I am not proud of the way in which I drew this distinction, and the fact that I saw things this way shows just how far off I still was from being any kind of feminist.

❁

The discipline of economics in India was marked in those days by a sense of urgency. The country was staggering under a sense of palpable economic malaise: the third Five–Year Plan would run into so many difficulties that the country would take a 'Plan Holiday' and resort to three Annual Plans during 1966–69. By the end of the Third Plan, the rupee was devalued, inflationary recession had set in; in 1964–65 and 1965–66, there was a severe drought and crop failure. In 1965, the country went to war with Pakistan, as a consequence of which the US, with no warning, cut food supplies, creating the acute food shortage that prompted Prime Minister Lal Bahadur Shastri's 'Miss-a-Meal'appeal to the nation to give up one meal a week.

It had become evident that effective policy changes and planned responses to the state of the economy required a precise measuring of economic activity that would demonstrate the relationship between different sectors of the economy. Even after the Third Plan, the country still hadn't achieved the desired economic goals. The models that had been tried had turned out to be ineffective and this created a sense of urgency in both the government and academia.

Delhi University at this time had an economist, B.N. Ganguli, as vice-chancellor, and several members of faculty with a keen interest in planning, public finance and welfare economics. There was K.N. Raj, who at twenty-six, had been the only professional economist in the team that formulated India's First Five–Year Plan. Then there was Sukhamoy Chakraborty, the development economist whose interest in planning can be gauged from his remark, 'If the First Five–Year Plan had not been published in 1951, the year when I opted to study economics, I would probably have studied philosophy.' Amartya Sen was beginning his work on welfare economics, and there was Jagdish Bhagwati, an expert on international trade.

I was fortunate to be there among them at that time. At the time that I joined Miranda House, there were very few lecturers who had a sufficiently strong background in mathematical statistics, and could teach public finance, especially since there was no prescribed textbook.

Interestingly, without knowing this, I had chosen these topics for my special papers in Oxford, as part of the PPE course. It was actually Peter Ady, also a developing countries' economist, who chose my topics according to the quality of the tutors. Paul Streeton was one of the greatest public finance economists and he was willing to take me for tutorials. Statistics was chosen because I had done advance papers in mathematics in India.

I would often stay in the home of Dr K.N. Raj as he and his wife Sarasamma and their two boys became very close friends. Amartya Sen was their neighbour and a few kilometres away were Sukhamoy Chakraborty and Lalita and on the other side of the road, Jagdish Bhagwati. The Delhi School of Economics was luminous. So staying with Raj or going to his house every evening after class gave me an opportunity to be with another kind of Mandarins. Raj was a magnet and people would drop by in the evening after their day's work. Sarasamma would provide coffee and something to eat and they would stay and talk for hours.

Another wonderful economist who was part of our group was Khaliq Naqvi. These 'addas' were a reflection of the political economy of the times. When P.N. Dhar, who was later to serve as Indira Gandhi's principal secretary in the tumultuous years of the Emergency, came from New Delhi to join us at the university, he brought a flavour of what the government was like. Then there was Pitambar Pant in the Planning Commission, another remarkable and brilliant economist.

While I lived in the university campus for short periods either with K.N. Raj or with Kanti Shastri, my home was with my brother Sreedhar who lived in Chanakyapuri.

Chanakyapuri and his life brought me in touch with those people who were part of the policitcal and official circles in what was called New Delhi, the seat of government. So I had an additional advantage that I could join my brother when he went to have dinner with Pitambar Pant and others outside the university circuit, like Romesh Thapar. Those years—1962–68—were years when I saw Delhi and India as an exciting open society where issues could be freely discussed and debated, and I had the good fortune of being part of that.

CHAPTER FIFTEEN

The Raj–Sen Impact

The decade of the 1960s was an era where not only were some of the best economists clustered together at the Delhi School of Economics, but there was a special subtext which was the bonding between K.N. Raj and Amartya Sen.

While they had very different areas of interest as well as academic journeys, their bonding was extraordinary. I think it arose from Amartya's deep respect for K.N. Raj as well as their background as Marxists. At that time one could not but have respect for Raj as he created his own intellectual outputs drawn from the ground, drawn from data, from agriculture and from poverty. These papers and lectures were so brilliant that it had earned him enormous respect from the academic fraternity apart from the government. He was the darling of Jawaharlal Nehru and was the author of India's First Five–Year Plan (1951–56).

During the 1960s, the Raj and Sen model, the Raj and Sen's articles, and finally, the Raj and Sen conflict was a strong intellectual space that academics and students were engaged in. It was my good luck and also very stimulating for me, that both of them were very dear friends—Sen, because we met as ex-Oxbridge people as far back as 1956, a friendship that has sustained because I was in Oxford again from 1958 to 1962 when Amartya was in Cambridge, and then later at Delhi University during 1962–67 at the same time that Sen was teaching at the Delhi School. Raj, I met not only in Delhi but in Oxford, where he came as a visiting scholar for a while in 1959.

Raj and Sen had many curious types of bonding. Both of them owned small blue Fiats. In fact, the Fiat was the most favoured small car in those days. I remember that because even Romila Thapar, another close friend, also had a Fiat in which I often used to get a lift from Chanakyapuri to Miranda House.

The Raj's blue Fiat had another story. K.N. Raj had an assignment in Washington, around 1964–65, and he asked me if I would like to use his car while he was away. I gladly accepted the offer as it really helped ease my daily commute from Chanakyapuri to the university. Plus, there was a bonus. Lakshmi and I had become lovers by then. I would drive the Fiat to the Safdarjung airport reception area, which in those days was much neglected. I would park and sit in the lounge and Lakshmi would come there in his white Ambassador and we would have an hour or so of companionship.

Before Raj returned, I had the little car fully overhauled and polished as a form of gratitude. One of Lakshmi's friends, also a great leader of the Cottage Industries, Suman Benegal, had a brother who was a car mechanic and worked at a petrol station or petrol bunk, as it was called in those days, in Chanakyapuri. She recommended him to me when I was looking for someone to repair the car and so when the car needed overhauling, I gave it to this young man. He not only did the overhauling, but a beautiful job of washing and polishing. When Raj returned he felt he could not recognize his car.

This experience led Raj to recommend a similar course of action to Amartya, who was then going abroad for a year with his wife, Nabaneeta and their first child, Pico. So the following year I had Amartya's car and apart from enjoying the freedom that it gave me, I also had it refurbished in many ways so that Amartya felt that I had given him a new car while he had given me an old one.

This closeness of the communities, whether at the university or in Panchampalli, as Sreedhar called the networks of Chanakyapuri and Pandara Road intellectuals, enriched my political engagement in those days.

❁

During these years, I was, I think, a popular teacher, and many of my students from that period have let me know of my influence on their future intellectual and political trajectories. I brought something of my experience of Oxford pedagogy to Delhi, setting them the advanced textbooks that were used in Oxford and instituting small tutorial-style teaching sessions to complement the larger lectures, a practice that made for a much more rigorous understanding of economic theory, and encouraged shy and under-confident students to speak up, express their opinions, and clarify what they did not understand. But my achievements up to that point were in the classroom, and I had little time or energy to devote to academic research.

Some time in the late 1960s, Raj and Romesh Thapar began to plan a special issue of their intellectual magazine,

Seminar, on the subject of 'the Indian woman'. Romesh's sister, Romila, who was then making waves as a historian of ancient India, persuaded me to contribute to that issue. I spent a while thinking about what I wanted to say, and then an old memory from childhood came back to me. My mother, I remembered, used to say some words of blessing whenever she gave her daughters an oil bath, the so-called 'panchakanya chiranjeevi': she would call on the ancient paradigms of female virtue and exhort us to emulate them. Ahalya, Tara, Sita, Draupadi and Mandodari, all good wives and daughters who either obeyed or, as in Draupadi's case, were forced to submit to the authority of the men in their lives, fathers and husbands. I saw them as women subdued by the patriarchy and I could no longer in good conscience accept them as models worthy of my emulation. I called in my article for a new panchakanya, for the celebration of more rebellious women in the tradition, women who stood up for themselves and didn't define themselves in relation to men: Amrapali, a cultured and worldly courtesan; Gargi, an ancient philosopher; Avaiyar, a Tamil poet and scholar, among others.

It was an unusual thing for me to do. My training in economics, and the syllabus I was teaching, didn't contain any special references to women's concerns, and I did not, at that stage, make any effort to bring them into my teaching. I was an enthusiastic teacher and tried to bring in several innovations in teaching methods, lecture design and delivery, based on my experience of studying at Oxford. I brought in more up-to-date textbooks and theories, and introduced a greater level of small-group teaching so that students didn't get lost in a large lecture theatre and both the bright and weak students could be encouraged to speak and ask questions. But feminism was no part of my innovations, until that article in *Seminar*.

Something in me shifted after that article. My essay was read by Sheila Dhar, the singer and writer who was then the director of the Publications Division (and the wife of P.N. Dhar). In 1974, she asked me if I would consider working on a book profiling the women of India, as part of the preparation for a pioneering international conference in Mexico on women. I agreed, and the book that came out of this commission, *Indian Women*, put me on a path away from the kind of economics I had previously been teaching. I became a very different sort of economist than I could have foreseen before I wrote it. The work, and the world into which it catapulted me, kept me breathlessly busy for the next four decades.

M.A. Sreenivasan and Singamma, Devaki Jain's parents, Bangalore, 1953, (above) and (below) a young Devaki with her grandmother and three aunts

tos: Courtesy Devaki Jain

A tomboy and a dancer: Devaki astride a horse, dancing at Harvard Square, 1958, (above) and (below) riding a cycle

Mount Carmel Convent, Bangalore, 1950, (above) and (below) Devaki playing the veena

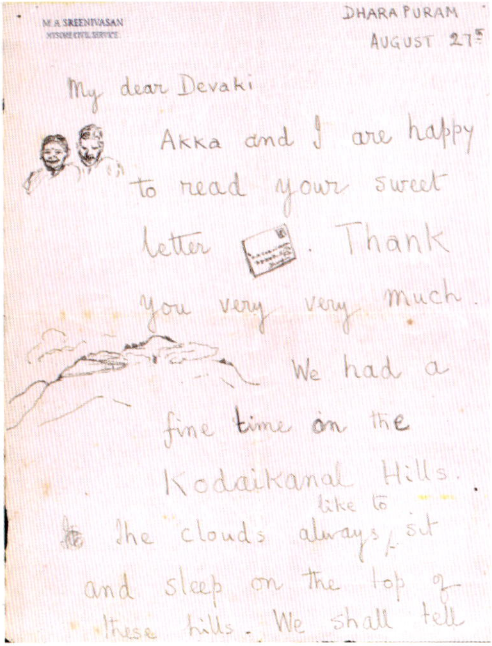
M A SREENIVASAN
MYSORE CIVIL SERVICE

DHARAPURAM
AUGUST 27th

My dear Devaki

Akka and I are happy to read your sweet letter. Thank you very very much.

We had a fine time on the Kodaikanal Hills. The clouds always like to sit and sleep on the top of these hills. We shall tell

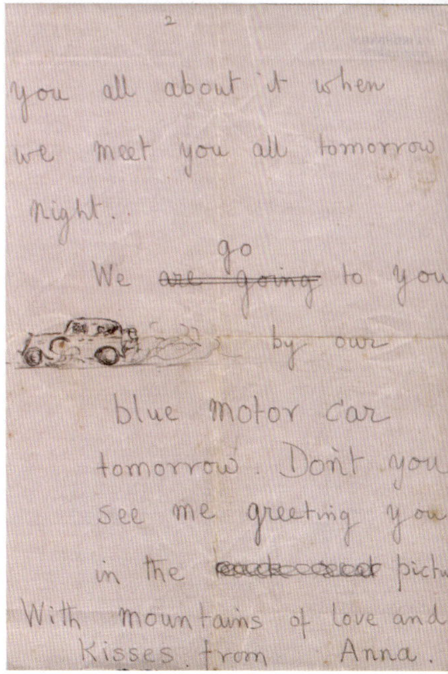
2

you all about it when we meet you all tomorrow night.

We ~~are going~~ go to you by our blue motor car tomorrow. Don't you see me greeting you in the picture

With mountains of love and kisses from Anna.

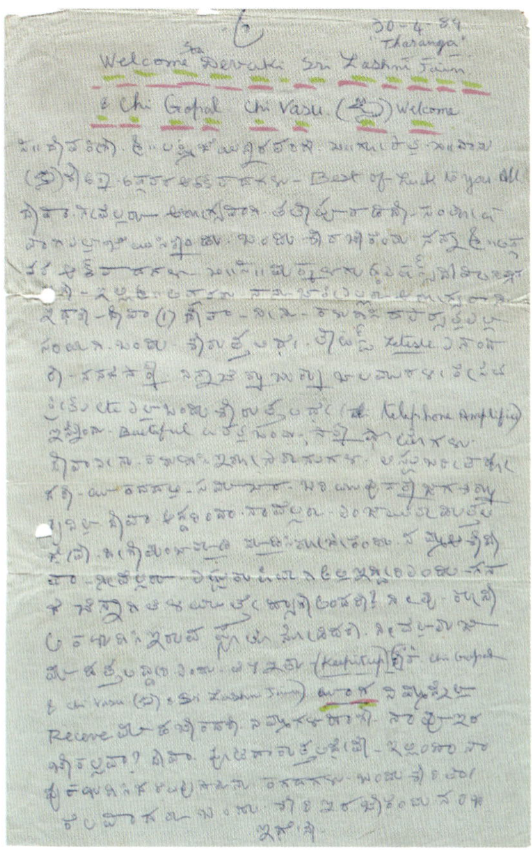
30-4-84
"Tharanga"

Welcome Sri Devaki Sri Lakshmi Jain & Chi Gopal Chi Vasu. Welcome

From Anna and Akka, with love: Letter to Devaki from her father (above) and (below) from her mother

Anna and Akka in New Delhi

Lufthansa
First Class Senator Service

Auf dem Flug
On the flight
En el vuelo
von/from/de nach/to/a

Sunday 8th July 1984

Our day

Beloved Devaki -

This is from your beloved

I could not have failed myself worse - and you could not have done more for me - to put me up

If I am, it's due to you. It will be trite to say thanks - even a million added to that will still be trite. But in the absence of another way of saying it - it's the only way. This morning though I did try to get across to you in whispering silence, my eternal gratitude.

We can handle life together in all its aspects joy and sadness. Negation of life - we still have to be on the same side of the fence - and yet the difference is not that much as it seems - because internally I sob and feel the stab

Yet some metaphysical force says "act as if the gone beloved is not gone - is still there", starting from Babaji, Mallick, Sudhir, Sridhar, ammaji, Kesari the inside is steeled. It still feels but the fear of wronging the one's loved one is so strong that more shaking the experience, more steady the feet.

Quite quietly akka took ammaji's place in the inside. The void was never felt by me, and she filled me with so much that I have yet to awake to the so called reality - and yet as I search myself I find myself enveloped by her and her love. How much she would have given that the thought of it gladdens my heart, I can't let grief take her place. It can't, I won't let it

I love you Lakshmi

Letter from Lakshmi Jain to Devaki, after her mother passed away

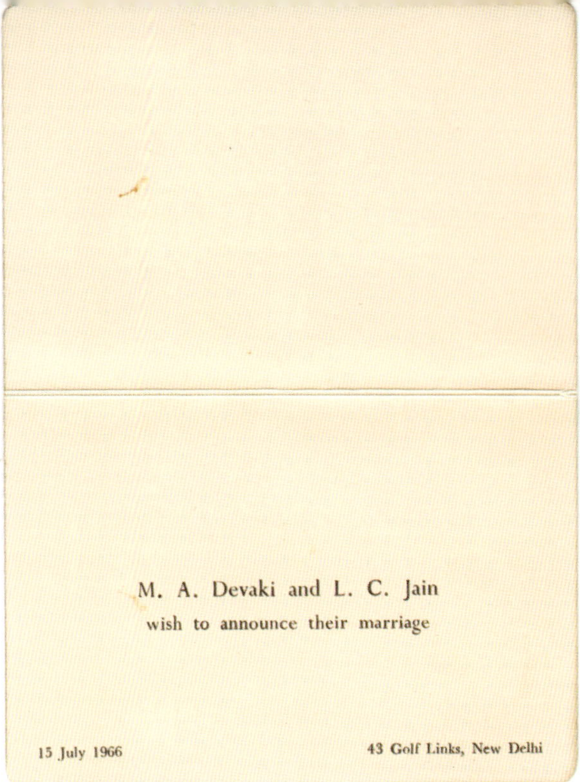

M. A. Devaki and L. C. Jain
wish to announce their marriage

15 July 1966

43 Golf Links, New Delhi

A wedding is announced: Devaki and Lakshmi Jain's wedding invitation (above)and (below) at their reception for colleagues at the Indian Cooperative Union, New Delhi, 1966

Comrades in arms: Lakshmi and Devaki Jain in New Delhi, 2008, (above) and (below) at their Jorbagh residence, 1976

Exploring new worlds: Devaki with women of colour, Harvard University, US, 1983, (above) and (below) with the DAWN group, Norway, 1984

Harvard, 1958: Devaki (top row, righthand corner) at a seminar organized by Henry Kissinger (seated fourth from left)

Flying high: With Fidel Castro in Cuba, as a member of the South Commission (above), and (below) with Alice Walker in Bangalore

Bonded by music: Devaki Jain with legendary vocalist M.S. Subbulakshmi

A dream comes home: Lakshmi Jain's swearing-in ceremony as Indian high commissioner in the Republic of South Africa, 1997. Nelson Mandela is second from left

A new dawn: Celebrating Freedom Day in Cape Town with Nelson Mandela (above) and (below) at a reception with Mandela and Graca Machel

Sharing a cause: With Dr Julius Nyerere (centre) in Cuba, 1989, (above) and (below) with Desmond and Leah Tutu, Pretoria, 1998

Woman of words: Devaki Jain at event for Lakshmi Jains' book 'Civil Disobedience and speaking at a seminar, (above) and (below) at a meeting of the South Commission group, China, 1989

PART SIX

Building New Worlds

'The most precious gift God gave humans is reason. Knowledge (science) is the best form of prayer.'

—Fatema Mernissi

CHAPTER SIXTEEN

Rethinking Economics

'I would like to believe that I earn my living honestly, but I often have doubts. I am concerned particularly for India and other developing countries whose economic doctrines come to them mainly from England and in English.'

—Joan Robinson, 'On Teaching Economics'

'If I wear my cloth over my shoulder like you upper-class women, will you clean my shit? Leave us alone. You do not want us to become strong. Then who will do your dirty work? We are doomed to labour forever,' screamed Thimmi, a Dalit woman from Chikmagalur in the state of Karnataka. She had a thin, torn piece of cloth on her body, wrapped under her arms and coming down to just below the knees. I was wearing a sari, draped around me, with the pallav thrown over my shoulders.

It was 1977, that eventful year. I was in Thimmi's village as part of a team along with the philosopher Ramachandra Gandhi, campaigning for the Janata Party, a new political formation that had come into being after the end of the state of Emergency that Indira Gandhi had declared two years earlier, suspending civil liberties and instituting press censorship. Lakshmi and I, and even our son Gopal, then ten years old, had been active in campaigning in that election, our house in Delhi turning into one of the centres of resistance, to the point that we were under constant police surveillance. We were all admirers of one of the leaders of the anti-Indira Gandhi movement, Jayaprakash Narayan, a socialist and Gandhian whose moral integrity had won him admirers from across the country, cutting across ideological divides.

Ramachandra Gandhi, my companion during some of my travels during that election, was a grandson of Mahatma Gandhi, and it was hoped by people in the Janata Party that his name might attract Dalit voters. In those days, the name of Gandhi was still associated with the emancipation and self-assertion of Dalits. (The move among Dalits away from Gandhi and towards Dr B.R. Ambedkar, a figure representing a different sort of politics and a more radical opposition to the caste system, occurred over the four decades since that election.) Ramachandra Gandhi respectfully asked Thimmi to vote for the Janata Party candidate, and it was then that she uttered those cutting words.

On a different occasion, this time while visiting a coffee-curing shed in Karnataka, I remember the words of Kempamma, a 45-year-old coffee worker, about her male supervisors at work. 'What do they know? We are to do nothing but bow our heads. I have a sick child, I am late, the family eats nothing that day, I bow my head. The union goes on strike, we starve for fifteen days, then are taken on for ten paise more in wages, and still I bow my head.' She suited the action to the word, like a swan disappearing into the water, all the while beating her forehead with her palm.

Then there was Fatima Bi. Fatima Bi lived in Delhi, in the area around the great mosque, the Jama Masjid, and was one of the many Muslim women there who did intricate embroidery in silver and gold thread. It was they who prepared the various decorations, palla, that adorned the mukuts, headdresses, worn by Hindu brides and grooms at weddings, and sold to them by the innumerable shops selling this kind of thing in the streets around Chandni Chowk. I remember arranging for her to visit the city of Ahmedabad where she found to her shock that the mukuts were being sold there at prices almost ten times as much as she sold the palla. She threw herself to the ground at the sight of the prices and, she later told me, beat her forehead to the floor, crying, 'Ya Allah! Is this what you call justice?' From that moment, she refused to put her hand to the needle till wages for her kind of embroidery were raised to a rate that better reflected the market value of her work. In a different context—a discussion of women callously divorced by their husbands, or having their incomes squandered by them—I remember another of her laments: 'Ya Allah! Mard kyon banaya?' Why did you create men?

These conversations were part of a pattern I have learnt over the years to see. Whatever the sector, female workers, despite working for hours every day with their hands, with a skill and physical effort no less than that of their male relations, and a commitment to cooking and childcare to which those men make no contribution, made very little money. Exploited by brokers and middlemen, little of the profit made on their work was reflected in what they were paid.

During my visit to the tea plantations in the hilly regions of Karnataka, female tea-pickers spoke of being continually propositioned by their male supervisors. Only those who agreed to provide sexual favours would have their bags of tea leaves weighed correctly, and therefore, be fully paid for the work they had done. Anyone turning down sex would have their bags deliberately underweighed. Economic exploitation—of which men were also victims—went hand in hand here with sexual exploitation.

I have related some of the aspects of my own experience—of abuse, harassment, direct and indirect discrimination—that made me receptive to the testimony of these women. But my work in the women's movement was in large part inspired, and later sustained by, my encounter with these women, with experiences of life, the economy and the patriarchy radically unlike mine. Thimmi, Kempamma, Fatima Bi—these were some of the women who taught me much of what I have since come to know about gender. They, more than any theorist, taught me my feminism. They have shaped the themes of my research and writing, provided much of its subject matter, and it is to them and others like them that I have always felt accountable.

I came to this kind of research relatively late in life. As I have said earlier in these memoirs, the early years of my career in university lecturing involved teaching a fairly traditional style of economics, the style then popular at Oxford and that formed the basis of the curriculum at Miranda House in Delhi. There was virtually no space in this for questions of gender, but I did not at that stage see this as a serious deficiency in the discipline. I took the discipline for what it was, and taught it with commitment and passion, but not, at this stage, with any critical angle on it.

In 1964, a group of economists from Harvard University and the Massachusetts Institute of Technology (MIT) came to India to carry out research in a village called Dhabi Kalan in Haryana. When I expressed interest in their fieldwork, they invited me to the village. I drove down with Romila Thapar, reaching the village in the evening. We were introduced to the family we were to stay with. As soon as we settled on the charpoys, the women started questioning us: were we married, they asked. When we said we were not, one of them came over and lifted my sari, putting her hand in between my legs! They could not believe women our age could be single and unmarried. They wanted to confirm that we were not men in the garb of women.

In 1969, I had to resign from my tenured lectureship at Miranda House, unable to cope with the care of my two infant sons at home, and the demands of a lively and fast-growing department of economics. My husband was more supportive than most people's, willing—as I have written earlier—to do the so-called Swedish swap and stay at home while I went to work. But I was unable to trust him, or anyone else, with the babies, on account of my own paranoia about their safety. With my full teaching load in the daytime and my childcare duties in the evenings, I felt out of touch with the cutting edge in economic research, simply from lacking the time in which to read regularly and engage with what was being published in the scholarly journals.

It was then, while I was still fretting at home in

1974, that Sheila Dhar called me and asked me to write a book replacing an earlier one called *Women of India from 1950*. She wanted the book in time for 1975, the year that the UN had declared as the International Year of Women. The work could be done at home, and was therefore manageable even with my neuroses. But I knew almost nothing of the subject.

It seemed too vast a domain for one person, however knowledgeable and hardworking, to handle in a year. I decided to make it an edited volume, in the hope that having several contributors might give the volume a comprehensiveness and internal diversity that one contributor could not achieve working alone. I cast a net over some of my academic and journalist friends and colleagues at the University of Delhi. I invited scholars such as Andre Beteille, Veena Das, Ashok Rudra, Romila Thapar and others to contribute to it, even if they had not previously written about women. I tried to draw them out from their disciplines and usual preoccupations and challenge themselves with new and fresh questions about the status of Indian women. I was also able to bring in friends from abroad such as Ester Boserup, whose work on women in African agriculture had been one of the first in her discipline to demonstrate the significance of gender roles in social analysis.

The volume (*Indian Women*) opened with an essay by Professor Ashish Bose, a demographer who was then a Fellow at Delhi University. He presented the sex ratio in India over a span of roughly seventy years, and the statistics were chilling indeed. From 972 females per 1000 males in 1901, the ratio had declined to 930 females per 1000 males in 1971. It was one of the early intimations of what would later become widely known: the practice of sex-selective abortions and female infanticide. This alone could account for the phenomenon that Amartya Sen would later make notorious with his phrase 'India's missing women'.

Other essays in the volume took on other topics: women who found strength in difficult, patriarchal rural environments; the paradox of a culture that venerated its goddesses but killed its baby girls. The novelist, Qurratulain Hyder, wrote a portrait of the lives of India's Muslim women. Women of many different kinds were described in the pages of the volume: nuns, teachers, nurses, students, matriarchs. The volume was released by the President of India in 1975, to commemorate the International Women's Year.

Until I threw myself into this book, I was, as I have said earlier, something of a 'queen bee'. My experiences so far had made me—or at least given me the ability to present myself as—a self-confident young woman unafraid of taking part in conversations with men on equal terms. I found the company of male colleagues at the university far more interesting than the women who, as I used to say mockingly, sat in the faculty room and talked of children's illnesses and how they had been awake all night. This while the men talked of game theory and Pareto Optimality, both of which I thought more congenial subjects. I should have known better, and it was only in the course of working on this book, finding myself exposed to lives vastly more deprived than mine, that I discovered just how much there was to learn, and how much there was to be done with that knowledge.

The declaration by the UN of 1975 as the International

Year of Women was not a merely symbolic gesture. It involved active measures and programmes, and a genuine attempt at initiating an international conversation on the subject of women and their condition. Governments were urged to step up and show that they were paying attention to the status of women in their countries. The Indian government set up a committee to report on the status of women in India. This report, titled 'Towards Equality', set out with clarity and force the aims that the growing women's movement would adopt as its own.

❁

My conversations with Professor Ashish Bose on his essay and the data it was based on pushed me into a new and unexpected direction. I had long had a hunch that the official figures on women's participation in work were seriously underestimating the facts on the ground; I also suspected that what lay behind this underestimation was a deep methodological flaw in the approach to measurement. As yet, this was a hunch, but Professor Bose's research inspired me to treat it as a hypothesis, and therefore, one that could be tested empirically and rigorously in a field-based study. I used the platform of a modest Delhi-based social sciences institute, the Institute of Social Studies, started by the distinguished economist, Professor Raj Krishna, and put in a proposal to the Institute of Social Studies Trust (ISST).

My proposal brought together two of my interests: my growing fascination with women's role in labour, and my specialisation in statistics, which I had studied to an advanced level as part of my course at Oxford and taught in the six years that I was a lecturer at Miranda House.

The grant enabled me to open a small office in a bedroom in our home in Jorbagh in 1976 to carry out this research.

The data bore out my hunch. The measurement was all wrong, and worse, much of the time, data on women's economic contribution was not even being collected. The problem lay in how the information was solicited, and at a subsequent stage, in how it was being coded. Another startling finding was that female work participation rates were in fact higher than participation rates for men amongst the landless in India (we used landlessness as a proxy for extreme poverty). This finding challenged the embedded view, taken for granted in most official statistics, that the main breadwinner of a household was generally a man.

The ISST study received widespread attention. We were invited to present our results at a number of conferences. It started what would become a lifetime's project, to learn about the myriad roles women occupied in the economy, and to develop methods of data collection adequate to the complexity of their involvement. In a phrase, it was all about counting correctly.

❀

Apart from challenging the data and the methodology of previous social science research, we at the ISST began to collect case studies of women who were coming together across traditional barriers of religion, language and caste to protect their interests, especially livelihoods. I put together, with Nalini Singh and Malini Chand, a volume titled *Women's Quest for Power: Five Indian Case Studies* (1980), bringing together some of the research that grew out of our initial concern with data collection. The book featured, and tried to bring attention to, several extraordinary collective organizations of poor and previously disempowered women. Over the years, while writing the book and later, we met, learnt from and often chronicled women in dairy cooperatives, women employed in making savoury snacks, women fighting male alcoholism, women trying to strengthen the bargaining power of self-employed workers, and women fighting eviction at the hands of municipalities by sleeping at their 'sales spots' under mosquito nets

My colleagues and I travelled extensively in those years, across the country, always on the look-out for stories that might serve as models and case studies that could be emulated elsewhere and inspire similar attempts at collective self-emancipation.

In the state of Mizoram, to take one example, women made coal and sold it in the local market. To make this coal they would walk down the slopes of Mizoram's mountains, cut tree branches and bring them up to char them into coal. But when I visited them, the supply of accessible branches was getting smaller and the women were having to walk deeper and deeper down into the valleys. Some of them had fractured or wounded their legs badly, needing to have them amputated or be unable to walk for the rest of their lives. This set me to look for ideas about alternative livelihoods for women who could no longer walk down the slopes, and to find alternative and less dangerous ways of making coal.

In the nearby northeastern state of Meghalaya, women had access to orchids, a natural growth, and turmeric and ginger of the most superb quality. But they could not access markets that enabled them to turn the availability of these natural resources into livelihoods for them. Wholesalers from the plains were buying up the material and selling it in the plains at huge profits, none of which was going back to the women. Noting these patterns, I designed and submitted a set of projects to the Planning Commission for funding, arranging for government departments to help these Meghalayan women to form cooperatives that would give them access to more of the profits from the orchids and spices they were growing.

We uncovered the tasks of women in various processes of production which had not been recognized and tried to get them included in any future accounts of production processes. In particular, we tried to get these tasks acknowledged when technological improvements were suggested, so that these improvements were not restricted to the tools and instruments used by men in the production process. This often had direct results for working women. For instance, some women working in the construction industry had lost their fingers or eyes in the course of breaking granite blocks into fragments, something that could be avoided if they were better equipped with tools and protective equipment.

In other cases, we drew attention to the costs of 'modernization' for women. We lived for three months in a coastal village to assess the impact on women of a new fish-landing harbour. It simply had not occurred to the project's designers that the livelihoods of women might be at stake, particularly of those hundreds of women who bought fish directly off the trawlers and then ran (to prevent the unrefrigerated fish from going bad) with the fish on their heads to villages in the interior to sell them. If policies were to be made on the basis of a cost-benefit analysis, then it was important to have the costs fully detailed. It was also important to know whether those who bore the costs were also those to gain from the benefits. I need not say that this was rarely the case.

Our interest in women and their work took us to sectors of the economy where women, by virtue of their supposed 'nimble fingers', were the sole workers. Peeling prawns without damaging them, dehusking cashew nuts, picking tea leaves, rolling bidis, rolling out papads, weeding fields, transplanting paddy, unseeding cotton pods: these were all delicate operations that required skill and experience to be done, and were crucial to the overall processes they were part of. But we found that the women were nearly always paid low wages despite how demanding the tasks were, and rarely covered by the protections in labour legislation.

These omissions had further consequences. I recall the raft of anti-poverty programmes introduced by successive Indian governments in the 1980s. Many of them operated on the principle of identifying households below the poverty line and offering them credit to enable them to upgrade their skills, or acquire an asset (for example, tools) to enable them to increase or supplement their income. Our research in this period attempted to get to the facts and experiences behind the abstraction of the poverty line, to break through the walls of these households to find out what was happening inside. We discovered here new omissions and distortions. The women in these households were generally assumed not to be taking part in any economic activity. But this was rarely the case. Even when the men in the household were, say, wage labourers, the women were rarely idle, or occupied exclusively with housework and childcare. They were often engaged in providing an additional income through selling cow dung cakes or rolling bidis, or something else that could be done from the home. But these women were almost never extended credit.

Something else we discovered was the danger of assuming the 'household' to be a single unified unit. Where there were scarce resources, such as food, this food would be given out sequentially: men and boys would be fed first and only then the women and girls. Sometimes there was almost nothing left for the girls to eat, and female family members were systematically less well-nourished than their brothers, fathers or husbands. Inequalities within inequalities, injustices within injustices, poverty within poverty.

Once we uncovered these patterns, we strove to bring it to the notice of that influential government body—at least in those relatively socialistic times—the Planning Commission. As a consequence, the Sixth Five–Year Plan (1985–90) had a separate chapter on women and the economy. It was progress of a kind, even if it did not then lead to any revolutionary change in the laws that applied to such workers.

We tried to bring more international attention to these discoveries—to the Food and Agriculture Organization in Rome, for instance—discoveries that were also being made by other economists with similar concerns in countries across the world. We urged them to qualify their notion that there could be such a thing as food security at the level of the household. We found this a complacent assumption. We urged the alternative formulation that household food security be understood in terms of the food security of the individuals within it, male and female.

The stories we found in the course of our field studies opened my eyes to a multitude of issues to which I had given little thought before: the sheer number of women workers, the low monetary and social value generally assigned to their work, the vulnerability of women in the workplace to every manner of exploitation, including sexual exploitation, no matter what the nature of their work. Watching them at work in their homes or plantations or shop floors and hearing them speak, I began to ask: are these women and the distinctive challenges they face part of the concerns of the mainstream in policy design? Are they being counted in the statistical system? Is their contribution to the Gross Domestic Product (GDP) being registered accurately? Are their problems being responded to by the monetary and fiscal instruments of the state?

In all this, the phrase I favoured to refer to the women I was working with and learning from was 'poor women'. The phrase sat uneasily with some of my colleagues and people otherwise sympathetic to what we were doing. The Marxists and socialists I knew thought the phrase was demeaning; others, more academically minded, saw in it the echo of some Dickensian world of workhouses and orphans. I myself did not find the word 'poor' problematic. Perhaps this had something to do with the Gandhian origins of my own thought, even if I did not go so far as some Gandhians and speak of 'Daridranarayana'—God seen in the poor. It seemed to me that there was no point concealing the reality behind euphemisms. These women were poor, but this did not call for pity but support, assistance, solidarity, and wherever possible, a change of policy. What we needed here was not new words but new nuances given to old words.

From the 1980s onward, I was continuously writing, talking and publishing about poverty and its special impact on women. This work drew the attention of policy-makers and the development community across the world. The eradication of poverty was one of the main priorities of the UN and similar bodies in the 1980s and 90s. My effort at all the meetings to which I was invited was to argue that poverty was the outcome of tolerating inequality, specifically, inequalities in power that allowed some people to become wholly dependent on others for the most basic necessities of life.

We in the women's movement in these years had begun to gender everything. Statistics, policies, institutions were the subjects of our critique. Soon, we tried for something more ambitious, to step in before the statistics were collected and policies devised and institutions designed so that they would not stand in need of a feminist critique later on.

In all this, my other perennial preoccupation has been to shift the focus of economics away from the GDP as a measure of development. I have not been alone in this, and the last few decades have seen several critiques of these approaches from philosophers, political scientists and economists alike. But this has not stopped media and governments from fixating on GDP growth as the true measure of a country and a society's development. One of the most striking, and accessible works on this subject that I know is the 1995 essay by three Yale economists,

Clifford Cobb, Ted Halstead and Jonathan Rowe: 'If the GDP is Up, Why is America Down?' They point out that the GDP grows from many things—for instance, a rise in the sale of home security systems, day care centres and diet pills. But these sales only show that society is fractured and mistrustful, parents overworked and people severely overweight.

I was never an influential academic economist. I left my university teaching post fairly early in my career, and my contributions to economics have come through non-traditional institutions. Sometimes I regret this. If my life had gone differently, if there had been more supportive institutions to allow me to balance my family commitments with the demands of an academic career, perhaps I too, could have published my work in the most elite journals. But when I look back on what I did instead, I find it hard to think that the work I actually did—field-based and directly oriented towards bringing about changes of policy—was of less value.

Without at first being aware that such a label existed, I became a feminist economist. That term can stand for a number of different projects. For me, it had started out as a systematic attempt to 'gender' data and projects, and more generally, to draw attention to and offer a critique of the gendered aspects of economic phenomena. But over the years, my approach in feminist economics went beyond this critical project to encompass the creation of new methods, approaches and analyses in economics; styles of economic reasoning that see beyond the world of men and the formal economy of companies and embrace the world of the informal economy with its more vulnerable participants; a 'bubble-up' economics, as opposed to the 'trickle-down' economics that has been so favoured in the last thirty or forty years. This alternative will certainly have gender at the heart of its analysis, but ultimately, the aim is a world without the stark inequalities of power that currently prevail.

Feminism as a term first entered my consciousness due to a deep and long friendship with Gloria Steinem. We met in 1958 in New Delhi, when she was still very far from being a feminist or part of the women's movement and neither was I.

Many years later it was both startling and thrilling, to find her face on the cover of an issue of the *TIME* magazine in 1971, with *Ms.* written on it and the narration of what this meant. She and her friends had launched an idea, an assertion of an identity, which was our own, not derived from men or marriage. The idea ran across the world with lightning speed.

I caught up with her again in 1974, when I visited the US, after a lapse of sixteen years. She introduced me to her colleagues in the *Ms.* magazine. The term 'feminism' was part of their language. It was all about organizing women into their own groups to enable collective strength in dealing with issues that confronted them. It was called 'feminist consciousness raising'. It was also about celebrating women. It was about inclusiveness—reaching out to those discriminated against due to race or colour. It was like raising our flag.

Though currently feminism is being claimed by so many diverse groups across the globe, each with its own story of its birth and its definitions, my entry was through the Gloria portal. We, Gloria and I, continue to swing together, even as we pass the ripe ages of eighty-five plus, due to the grounding and belief in feminism and non-violence.

Gloria introduced me to Alice Walker. She took me with her to watch the opening in New York of the stage presentation of *The Colour Purple*, a programme pulled together by Oprah Winfrey. Alice introduced the programme and then came down to sit with us in the audience; she was wearing a long dress more like a monk's robe. So there were four of us—Gloria, Oprah, Alice and myself sitting together watching the first show of the dramatization of *The Colour Purple*.

Many years later, I had the privilege of visiting Alice and even staying in her house in California as a guest, in 2014. She encouraged me to write my own story and so I started the first page in the basement of her house, which was a big apartment for guests. Alice and I took long walks on the beach and drove through the woods. She is perhaps the most sensitive and the most philosophical writer in the world today and I love and admire her.

I particularly like her nuancing of the idea, feminism. In an interview taken by Rudolph Byrd, she says: 'As long as the world is dominated by racial ideology that places whites above people of colour, the angle of vision of the womanist, coming from a culture of colour, will be of a deeper, more radical penetration. This is only logical. Generally speaking, for instance, white feminists are dealing with the oppression they receive from white men, while women of colour are oppressed by men of colour as well as white men, as well as by many white women. But on the joyful side, which we must insist on honouring, the womanist is, like the creator of the word, intent on connecting with the earth and cosmos, with dance and song. With roundness, thankfulness and joy. Given a fighting chance at living her own life, under oppression that she resists, the womanist has no or few complaints. Her history has been so rough—captured from her home, centuries of enslavement, apartheid, etc—she honours Harriet Tubman by daily choosing freedom over the fetters of any internalized slavery she might find still lurking within herself. Whatever women's liberation is called, it is about freedom. This she knows. Having said this, I have no problem being called "feminist" or "womanist." In coining the term, I was simply trying myself to see more clearly what sets women of colour apart in the rainbow that is a world movement of women who have had enough of being second– and third–class citizens of the earth. One day, if earth and our species survive, we will again be called sacred and free. Our proper names.'

A rich expansion which I totally endorse.

CHAPTER SEVENTEEN

Upturning Hierarchies

'Allah made the earth a carpet for you so you can travel...'

—Fatema Mernissi

'She has wheels on her feet': I think this phrase is used in several Indian languages to describe women who are constantly travelling ('kaalile chakram' in my own language, Tamil). The phrase sometimes carries with it a sense of exasperation or dismissal: why can't she stay in one place? I was just the sort of person to whom that phrase applies. In retrospect, it amazes me to find that over a span of about fifty years, starting 1955, I have travelled to ninety-four different countries. I have also had the privilege of visiting every one of the twenty-nine states and seven Union Territories in India. In most of them, I have visited some of the poorest and most marginalized villages to meet women and to try to understand their struggles. Very little of this travel was for tourism or holidays. Nearly all of it was professional travel with my costs covered.

This cycle of constant travel began in a sense in

childhood, when I accompanied my father on his trips and safaris. So many of my memories of childhood are of me in the back seat of a car, en route to somewhere unfamiliar. But I really became a self-sufficient traveller in my own right in 1962, when I found myself part of an unusual, and now almost impossible, overland trip from Oxford to Delhi. The leader of this bold travelling party was Elizabeth Whitcombe, an Oxford student who had studied 'Greats': that is to say, the four-year degree in Greek and Latin languages, literature, history and philosophy. She had only two conditions for members of her party: one had to be able to drive, and to contribute £100 to the kitty. In the end, there were four of us: two men and two women in a hardy Land Rover.

We started, of course, from where we were, in Oxford, and took the ferry across the English Channel into France. We drove across France and Switzerland, all the way down to Greece and then Turkey. Throughout, we stayed in what were called 'mocamps'—camps for motorists to park their cars and spend the night. Sometimes, we slept out in the open in our sleeping bags. Elizabeth, a seasoned camper who had climbed mountains in New Zealand, brought all the necessary equipment. A well-read scholar, she could educate us about the antiquities in Greece and Turkey—archaeological sites and ancient monuments—that we visited.

From Ankara in Turkey, we went on through Trebizond, Batumi, Erzurum, Tabriz, stopping in each town, walking through and occasionally shopping in the bazaars. We all bought leather coats in the market in Istanbul, where the sturdiest and cheapest leather goods were to be found. The one memory of that part of the trip that stayed with me as a traumatic experience was seeing the decapitated heads of cattle being used to hang things on—bags, hats and so forth. The heads still had eyes and it was like they were staring right back at me when I looked at them.

One of my co-travellers, a mathematician from New Zealand called David Vere Jones, wrote to me recently with some of his memories from this leg of the journey: of a mosque with a wooden floor and many squares of old carpets, of leaving the mosque after dark in search of a camping ground, of eventually settling down for the night in a dry riverbed where some nomads were camping opposite. Some of the children and old men in their encampment came to visit us, bringing us melons; we accepted gratefully, offering them cigarettes and brandy in return. They sang for us, and one old man chose a particularly bawdy number that sent his companions into convulsions of laughter. David can also remember swimming in lakes, and the constant stomach upsets to which we all fell prey during the journey.

We had a minor accident while driving in Turkey (I'm afraid I was the driver responsible!). I overturned the Rover so that one of its doors came unhinged. We were all wounded. We were in urgent need of an opportunity for rest and recuperation, and my brother Rajan came to our rescue. He was then joint secretary in the Ministry of Information and Broadcasting in New Delhi and used his connections in the diplomatic services to come to the aid of his adventurous sister. One of his friends, Rashid Ali Baig, was the Indian ambassador to Iran at the time and he was alerted to our presence in the country. So we landed, wounded and a little shaken, at his door. In their usual gracious and hospitable fashion, he and his wife

Tara took us in and let us stay with them for ten days while we recovered and had proper hot baths, while they confided in us about the political situation in the country, to which they had a special access as diplomats from a friendly country.

Rested now, we continued on to Meshed and then—what now seems incredible—to Kabul, and then across Pakistan to end, as we had planned, in Delhi. Knowing what I now know of Afghanistan's unhappy subsequent history, I find it difficult to believe that we slept out on camp beds, waking every day to the fresh mountain air and the singing of birds. We met no extremists, dressed as we liked, crossed no minefields, and encountered no homicidal American drones. Sometimes, I wish one of us had taken a camera, or that I had kept a diary of the trip. It simply did not occur to me to do so. The idea had been to live it, not to use the trip to accumulate material for subsequent reminiscences.

My overland journey was perhaps the most adventurous travelling I ever did, but it came a few years after a journey that had been just as stimulating. This was a trip to the US I made after being one of two Indians selected for a programme at Harvard University by a man then largely known for his academic achievements: Henry Kissinger. His reputation as a foreign policy strategist and his role in the Vietnam War and in the Richard Nixon administration was still many years away at the time I was acquainted with him.

The programme that Kissinger ran aimed to identify and bring together, for a three-month seminar, people aged between thirty and fifty, with the potential to be influential leaders. I was twenty-five, and well below the average age of participants in this programme. Kissinger later told me that my application impressed him not because of the extent of my experience but because of its conviction. I had written with passion of Vinoba Bhave's bhoodan movement in India—the attempt to persuade landowners to give their land voluntarily to the landless. I had found the idea compelling the moment I heard of it and took part in it (as I have briefly mentioned in previous chapters) in the years after I returned to India after my time at Ruskin College.

At Harvard, I was an active participant in discussions that mostly involved people older than me. Kissinger, it turned out, appreciated my contributions and asked me what else I might like to do while I was in the US. I replied, somewhat boldly, that I wanted to do three things: to travel to the southern states of the US and meet anti-racist campaigners and people active in the civil rights movement; to visit the best departments of economics in the country and listen to the conversations being conducted there; and to return to India not the way I had come (via London) but via the Pacific route. I was granted a scholarship by an institution called the Asia Foundation to enable my travel. Kissinger used his academic influence to get me introductions to scholars in a number of American universities.

I used the scholarship to go to Atlanta, in the state of Georgia. When there, I lectured on Gandhi and his methods of satyagraha at an all-black college called Hampton Institute. From there, I went on to South Carolina and here, I had the enormous good fortune of meeting Rosa

Parks over dinner: Parks was the pioneering figure of the civil rights movement whose defiant act of refusing to give up her bus seat to a white man in Alabama in 1955 had, effectively, inspired the movement—one of its early successes was to have racial segregation on public buses ruled unconstitutional. I wish I could remember the subjects we conversed about, but the memory of being in her presence looms larger than anything in particular we said to each other.

Throughout these travels, I experienced something that I have found always marks social movements: people involved in it are deeply concerned to make themselves and the justice of their cause understood to outsiders. The need for people who express solidarity with one's cause is, I think, a deep human need. Every meeting during these travels seeded another and I was rarely without an introduction to someone who was ready to walk and talk with me, telling me things about the movement that I could not possibly have got from reading a book. I found myself, a little while later, marching with the leaders of the National Association for the Advancement of Colored People (NAACP) in Harlem, a black-majority area of New York City.

I proceeded then to a tour of American university campuses: Chicago, then on the west coast, Berkeley and Stanford. In all of these places, I had the good fortune of meeting prominent economists who were the flavour of the month on their campuses as writers of important recent monographs; many of them were kind enough to come to meet me at the airport and accommodate me while I was there.

My way back to India took me first to Hong Kong,

then to Tokyo—where I stayed at the home of a family called the Yoshidas, to whom I was introduced by a man called Bill Clifford, an editor at Random House, who had published the novelist R.K. Narayan, whose family I had known in Mysore. The Yoshidas were makers of wood block prints and their lifestyle was deeply Japanese: the design of their house, the doors, the hard beds and the communal bath where the matriarch of the family had to teach me to bathe. One of her artisan sons, Toshi, later rose to great fame, travelling across the world making presentations at international museums on traditional Japanese block prints.

I went on to Cambodia and found a journalist who was driving in a jeep to visit the awe-inspiring ruins of Angkor Vat. It was, in those days, still largely jungle and the tall figures in the temples and other buildings were intertwined with the trees. (I visited the ruins again in 2006 and found to my disappointment that the place had lost most of its romance after it had been cleared and made ready for tourists.)

Finally, I arrived at Rangoon (present-day Yangon) where I managed to get an appointment with Burma's minister for planning, and even managed to get my hands on a copy of the Burmese five-year plan—a document that would come in useful during my time working as a research assistant at Oxford on a project on Asian economies.

❁

This travel was a prelude to the travelling that comprised a substantial part of my working life, particularly my work in development policy and as part of my participation in the international women's movement. Specialized international agencies, such as the International Labour Organization or the Food and Agriculture Organization, were in constant need of people who were familiar with academic economics, policy and grassroots activism, and were willing to travel. The liveliness of the women's movement and the institutions with which I was then involved led to a constant stream of invitations to me and my colleagues to travel, lecture, serve on committees and so forth.

I went to such places as Fiji as a member of the UN's regional office for women and development, but I made sure on each occasion to go beyond the official committee meetings and learn something of the culture I was visiting. One of my most vivid memories of that trip to Fiji was my boat ride, shuttling down the rapids at a high speed and feeling the terrifying rush of water all around me. It had all the excitements of my youthful horse riding and an added layer of danger.

Another such visit was to the island of Tonga in the south Pacific, southeast of Fiji. What struck me most was not the strangeness of the people I met but their utter familiarity. They looked to me uncannily like Keralites; their lower garments were draped in the style of the Kerala dhoti and they ate off large leaves with their fingers, sitting cross-legged on the ground. It was amazing how easily I could join in their life despite coming from a country so far away.

On these travels, I usually focused on women's work, learning slowly by patient observation what the existing discourse, in academia and in policy circles, was lacking. The available vocabulary to describe economic phenomena, I found, was seriously impoverished, unable to capture important features of what I was observing in India and other countries in the global south. This misnaming was not a minor linguistic point. The erroneous naming and description of economic phenomena had direct consequences for a number of important things. I frequently saw projects designed at solving the wrong problems and funding allocated inefficiently or wastefully simply because we lacked a vocabulary to describe the conditions that these projects were supposed to be addressing. My term for this phenomenon, 'the oppression of vocabulary', caught on among activists, encouraging theoretical work that aimed to find terminology adequate to the phenomena.

A similar mistake in nomenclature was the labelling of the larger part of the workforce in countries like India as 'informal' workers (the formal workforce consisted of those who worked in factories with regular wages). But 'informal' suggests, what is untrue, that this sector is unregulated and not bound by anything other than loose and ad hoc rules. This is simply false. A good deal of work in the informal sector is in fact subcontracted and contractors have extremely severe rules and systems in how they employ labour. Again, terminology can distort our perception of the phenomena.

The problem is not only, as we might say, epistemological. The distortion of the phenomena by preconceptions or poor terminology translated into bad policy. I can remember a United States Agency for International Development (USAID)-funded programme for India in the 1950s, later developed by the United Nations Food and Agriculture Organization into a general approach towards rural women. Funding was directed towards training men in agricultural science while women were given training in 'domestic' science and 'home economics'. This gendered division of funding reflected the view, quite mistaken, that men in a traditional society like India, being cultivators, were likelier to benefit from agricultural science than women, who stayed at home. But this simply did not correspond to the facts. Women were themselves heavily involved in agricultural labour and were just as much in need of training in modern agricultural science as the men.

On my various trips abroad as a representative of 'third world women', I began to notice a disturbing, but entirely predictable, pattern. These meetings always involved technocrats, usually male and from the countries located in the northern hemisphere, and the home of the colonizers. These experts took it upon themselves to simultaneously define their terminology, describe the experiences of people from everywhere in the world, and to prescribe solutions. They were there to teach, we to learn; they didn't seem to think they had anything to learn from us, or we anything to teach them. I can remember one such meeting, in Copenhagen, as part of the preparation for a UN conference to be held in 1980. There were fifteen of us women present, all from the south, that is, from the southern continents, mostly nations that had been colonized. The convener began to list the proposed projects and to ask us for our approval. There was an uncomfortable silence in the room and we women exchanged significant glances. It wasn't that we had nothing to say, but that we didn't know where to start.

The approach being set out, with its confident assumptions about what our countries needed, was simply not reflected in our own conceptions of what we needed. More than this, there was a strong sense of a power relation: they were there to give us authoritative advice. We were allowed, at best, to make constructive suggestions to help to put their ideas into practice. We were not expected to offer a fundamental critique. But a fundamental critique is what was needed. When we left the meeting, we had the chance to articulate this feeling to each other.

Things were not all gloomy, and not everyone I met at these conferences took the same attitude. Our Scandinavian sisters turned out to be sympathetic to our concerns once we began articulating them. They did genuinely care for what we had to say and listened closely to us, often visiting us and our movements in our countries, trying to see what the official reports written by economists and statisticians were leaving out. On one such visit, the leader of the Swedish Women's Development department (SIDA), Karin Himmelstrand, asked me for my advice on what they should be doing in Nairobi at the UN's World Women's Conference in 1985. What should they fund? What events should be organized?

I took the liberty of saying what I had felt ever since the uncomfortable meetings in Copenhagen. We, women of the south, I told her, were uncomfortable with the patronising assumptions of our northern colleagues as they were expressed in the latter's research, analyses and conclusions. The constant assumption that we were all poor and illiterate, trapped in archaic cultures and conventions, in need of being rescued by modern institutions, ultimately embodied the invisible claim of cultural and political superiority. They replicated the basic logic of colonialism. Not only did this conceal the enormous complexity and diversity of our societies, it had the function of suggesting, quite falsely, that women in prosperous northern societies were not themselves oppressed by features of their cultures and conventions, failed by their institutions and in need of better access to money, power and education.

Himmelstrand invited me to address the Women in Development (WID) group of the Organization for Economic Cooperation and Development (OECD), at their pre-Nairobi meeting in 1983. My lecture at this event, 'Development as if women mattered: Can women build a new paradigm?' analyzed more than a hundred reports of what were called 'North–South' transfers of funds for WID projects, and argued that virtually all of them had either no impact, or a negative impact, on poor women simply because their roles had not been accurately identified so that the funds might be more intelligently used directly for their benefit. I circulated this lecture to some of the women I had met on my travels or with whose work I was familiar from each continent of the south. I sent it to Fatema Mernissi from Morocco, Marie-Angélique Savané from Senegal, Hameeda Hossain from Bangladesh, Noeleen Heyzer from Malaysia, Neuma Aguiar and Carmen Barroso from Brazil, Peggy Antrobus from the Caribbean, Lourdes Arizpe from Mexico and Claire Slatter from the Fiji Islands. I was pleased to find that each one of them saw the truth in my argument and were willing to identify themselves with my contentions.

I organized a meeting in Bangalore the next year—in August 1984—to discuss and debate our 'Alternative'. In three intense days of discussion and constructive debate, the Bangalore group transformed the UN's framework for the Nairobi conference that was to be held in 1985.

The UN had sent a questionnaire to help countries prepare for Nairobi that was based on what we feminists called the 'ladders approach'—one that measures the disparities between men and women in a select set of indicators such as education, employment and health, and then works to bring women up to the same level as men as a way of achieving equality. It was a linear framework and did not engage in any analysis of the links between status and macro policies; it was not related to the reality on the ground or the downflow of the macro forces.

The Bangalore group struggled to fit their issues within this framework for Nairobi. When we were torturing ourselves on how to get into the framework that the UN had given all the countries, one of my invitees, Fatema Mernissi, just lost her cool, got up and in a typical loud Fatema way said, 'Tear off all those charts you have pasted on the walls, this is trapping our minds. Let us look at our continents and identify our crises and then shape our reports accordingly.'

I first met Fatema Mernissi at a seminar in Harvard in 1983, in a dialogue across faiths. She was so lit up—vivid, articulate, argumentative and fun-loving. She had brought a music CD for belly dancing and she would dance for us in the evenings. Mernissi was a historian teaching at the Mohammed V University in Rabat. To Mernissi, knowledge was the critical element in building peace and understanding. She talked incessantly of the

Sufi scholars who walked across Africa and Asia to take back the knowledge learnt on their travels. Violence, she believed, was engendered by ignorance, and symbols such as 'Sindbad the Sailor' and the 'Flying Carpet' could help overcome antagonisms.

Mernissi had the most innovative ways of explaining symbols. One time, when she decided to call an initiative 'The Casablanca Dream', the head of the United Nations Development Programme in Rabat—a fine European—smiled sardonically and said: 'But you do know that dreams are too much like vapours? It is not reality if you call that project Casablanca Dream.' Mernissi raised her body to her full height and beauty and retorted: 'No, sir, dreams, in our view, are the most creative experience in our life. It is in dreams that we capture new ideas and learned thoughts.' Similarly, to her, the 'Flying Carpet' was the journey of the mind across differences, and 'Sindbad the Sailor' was someone learning to relate to the other, to understand the other, all to diffuse antagonisms.

At the Bangalore conference, Mernissi shocked all of us when she said: 'This is not the way to think—against someone else's framework...let us start from ourselves.'

We went around the room identifying the major concern in each continent. The group quickly identified the crises in its regions: Africa's food crisis, Latin America's debt, South Asia's poverty and the militarization of the Pacific Islands. Poor women in these regions were not only totally engaged in the economies of these countries but were suffering from and responding creatively to these onslaughts.

A new framework began to emerge—one that linked the situation of poor women to the macroeconomic and political framework of their countries and regions. We described how the problems of food, debt, militarism and religious fundamentalism affected them, and explored how these experiences could be captured in panels at the Nairobi conference. We chose a title for our project: Development Alternatives with Women for a New Era. The acronym, DAWN, symbolized for all of us a new start, a new path. DAWN went on to present five panels at Nairobi.

Around the same time, the Non-Aligned Movement (NAM)—a movement of countries, many of them former colonies of European powers, who were not aligned either with the US or the Soviet Union—held its first, I think its only, ever conference on women in Delhi. At the height of its power and influence, NAM had a certain amount of power and moral authority and was trying to carve out a space for itself in international politics. The conference was held in part out of a desire to produce a document and a coherent position that could be presented at Nairobi, representing the voice of women from former colonies. I was an official delegate to this conference, aiming to make as many allies for our cause as we could persuade to share our vision. I shared with the delegates what was going through our minds as women scholars and activists and befriended the remarkable woman who was the inspiration and intellectual lead for that conference, Vida Tomšič.

Many years later, in the early 2000s, I was commissioned to contribute to a series of books chronicling the intellectual history of the United Nations. I was asked to write about the history of women within the UN. The process of researching this book provoked the same kinds of discontent in me: it was frustrating to see just how Eurocentric the periodization of history was. Even in an essentially international body like the UN, the categories of 'pre-war' and 'post-war' were often used without question. This was understandable, as the Second World War was, of course, an important factor in the birth of the UN. But other dates were much more significant in the countries of the global south: pre- and post-apartheid, for instance, or pre- and post-Independence (as in the cases of most former colonies). Once we went further back into the past, the most important explanatory categories for the societies of the north were not wars and diplomacy, the stuff of mainstream histories, but such long-term processes as slavery and indentured labour. In a country like India, the thoughts of Mahatma Gandhi and B.R. Ambedkar had much more to offer us than someone like John Maynard Keynes.

I took the writing of the book as a chance to redress this imbalance somewhat. I did not mince words in offering my critique of the UN's many agencies, challenging the unreflective reference to women in our countries as having no agency (until some UN agency thought to give us some), as being enslaved and subordinated and in need of foreign liberators. Even when these agencies were run by people with the best of intentions, it was difficult to free the agencies from the basic assumptions that came of it being dominated by people and ideas from the former colonizers. I remain largely pessimistic about the UN: there are limits to what it can do to offer fundamental criticisms of government policy as long as it remains an institution dependent for its funding and legitimacy on the countries of the north.

Still, the UN, its agencies and its conferences, allowed for a range of conversations between movements in different parts of the world that could not have come together in any other way. Even if the UN itself does not transform into a truly progressive or radical body, it can still create spaces and possibilities for other people and institutions to offer a radical critique of international institutions, including the UN itself. This is the role it has played in my own life, and I can name many other people in the international women's movement who are grateful to the conversations and solidarities it made possible.

CHAPTER EIGHTEEN

Claiming Histories: Claiming the South

It was at this time, in the mid to late 1980s, that I made a new and important acquaintance. I had been organizing a meeting of significant achievers from across the southern continents to address the question of indigenous wisdom: how might practices that were native to our own countries help us to define a vision of development that was not merely imposed on us by technocrats from abroad? Once I had raised the funds, I began to look for a well-known and sympathetic figure to inaugurate the conference and thereby give it international visibility. This was when I was first introduced to Dr Julius Nyerere (1922–99).

Nyerere was the man who had led Tanganyika to independence in 1961 and, shortly afterwards, negotiated a union with Zanzibar, thereby creating the new state of Tanzania, whose president he was from 1964 to 1985. He was a remarkable reader, his reputation in Africa much like that of Gandhi in India. He, too, was deeply committed to non-violence and his life's mission had been to nudge people away from violence in their struggles and to create an Africa whose newly liberated nations would be committed to justice rather than vengeance.

When I first came to know him, he had just been

appointed, by leaders of the Non-Aligned Movement, chairperson of something called the South Commission, constituted to give voice to the shared perspective of the south, drawn from the experience of our own countries, not simply imported from northern models that may not be suited to the conditions in our societies. I first met Dr Nyerere in a large drawing room in a New Delhi hotel in 1986 when he was in India looking for people to serve on the commission.

He was a trim, fresh-looking man. He had salt and pepper hair, closely cut but curly. He was in the standard bureaucrat's ensemble: a safari suit over a bush shirt. His shoes were extremely well polished. He always looked like this in all the time I knew him, everything about him crisp and just so. I asked him whom he had recruited to the commission so far, and his answer was just as I had expected: retired or senior politicians, bankers, administrators, civil servants. There were few representatives of civil society, people from outside the political-bureaucratic establishment, virtually no scholars or academics, and of course, no women. My reaction to his list was the unrehearsed exclamation: 'What are you doing with a commission of old men?'

Other people in his position could have ignored me, or taken offence. He did neither. 'Joan!' he shouted. A woman emerged from one of the doors at the side of the hotel room. She was small, a little hunched and had a mop of grey hair with the slip-on 'pump' shoes typical of the serious Englishwoman. 'Yes?' she asked.

'She,' said Dr Nyerere pointing to me, 'says that I have put together a bunch of tired old men in the commission.' Far from being offended, he laughed uproariously.

Joan Wicken was an Oxford 'girl' from a working-class background, a graduate of Somerville College, who had been so moved by what she had read of the movements for national liberation in various African countries that after graduating from university, she travelled there to volunteer her skills. It was then that she came into Nyerere's orbit and became indispensable to him by typing up his speeches at political meetings, writing up the minutes of the meetings, and later, moved into his secretariat. When he retired from the presidency of Tanzania, she decided to accompany him on his new role as chairman of the South Commission.

She was a wonderful woman, bright and dedicated, and Dr Nyerere trusted her implicitly. Later that evening, when I got back to my home in Old Delhi, a long way from the fancy hotels of New Delhi, I heard her voice at the other end of the phone: 'Mwalimu wants you to join the South Commission. He needs an answer right away: the Government of India is proposing other names, and he needs to reply to them shortly.' She used the name for Nyerere by which people across Africa knew him: Mwalimu, or 'teacher' (he had been a teacher before he entered politics, but the word also captured a deep feature of his temperament and personal manner).

I was stunned and turned to Lakshmi, who was standing next to me. He didn't need a moment to think about it: 'Accept the invitation,' he whispered, 'it will be a privilege to work with him.' I did, and thus became the first woman to join the South Commission. Later, two other women were brought in: a colleague of mine from the DAWN group, Marie-Angélique Savané of Senegal, and Solita Collás-Monsod, an economist from the Philippines. We were the only three women in a commission with twenty-eight members. I should add that in the end, Dr Nyerere wasn't able to inaugurate the meeting on indigenous wisdom—of such accidents is a life made!

❁

The ambitions of the South Commission had emerged in part from a contrast from two similar bodies whose work in the 1970s and 80s amounted to a vision of the political economies of the north, the colonizers as well as the US. The Brandt Commission (1977–80) and the Brundtland Commission (1983–87) had effectively shown the political and economic features that unified the countries of the north: the relative contributions of agriculture and industry, industrial relations, trade unionism, levels of mechanisation etc. Despite all the differences between their economies, these countries had a great deal in common and these commissions brought out these commonalities with great insight. It led to the founding of the European Union, and the Economic Commission of Africa (ECA), and forged a solidarity which led to collective negotiations with the 'other'. This made a big difference to the economic power and health of these countries.

As Nyerere later observed in an incisive speech made in Belgrade in 1989, 'We cannot pretend that the north does not exist. It is powerful and it makes decisions that affect the south. The market economy countries of the north increase their already great strength by meeting on a regular basis and before any major international conferences. They dominate the world economy, and use its institutions to promote their own interests.' Changing this would require that the south find an accurate self-understanding, and the South Commission aimed to give to the countries of the south a self-understanding adequate to their shared needs. But a sense that our countries did have shared needs was itself something that needed to be created and fostered. As the Working Party on South–South Cooperation declared in 1988, 'The south is essentially a project, an idea in the making.'

The commission did not by any means take a merely antagonistic attitude to the countries of the north, even when that category included former imperial powers whose policies had a great deal to do with the immiseration of the countries of the south. But it was clear to all of us that we were not beholden to those countries, and certainly did not intend to defer meekly to them and their technocrats, however much wealth and power they possessed. Dr Nyerere himself was motivated by moral conviction. At a meeting in London in 1975, he had made a powerful declaration: 'In one world, as in one state, when I am rich because you are poor, and I am poor because you are rich, the transfer of wealth from rich to poor is a matter of right.'

This intellectual and political self-confidence was clearly reflected in the personal and political style of Dr Nyerere. He was a devout Christian but steeped in his native culture and folklore. His speeches were dotted with parables and proverbs from Swahili. His speech at the formal inauguration of the South Commission in Geneva in October 1987 was a memorable occasion. He told his audience, largely composed of diplomats and other bureaucrats, of an exchange between a rabbit and an elephant (I quote a part of it from memory):

O rabbit, rabbit, where are you going?
 I am going to kill the elephant.
But rabbit, he's so big and strong!
 Well, I'll try, and try again.

This was his constant refrain: let us try. Let us not be overwhelmed by the power of the former colonizers. Liberation from colonization meant little, he argued, unless we had liberation from economic exploitation and domination. The other members of the commission had many disagreements with Nyerere, but few were immune to his charisma.

Over the course of the process, members of the commission had to travel constantly. We went to ten countries, conferring with the leadership and with intellectuals. We began with a meeting in Mont-Pèlerin, Switzerland; for the rest of the meetings, we kept away from western Europe: Kuala Lumpur, Malaysia; Cocoyoc, Mexico; Kuwait; Maputo, Mozambique; New Delhi, India; Nicosia, Cyprus; Havana, Cuba; Caracas, Venezuela, and finally to Nyerere's own country, Arusha, Tanzania. The commission had the chance to conduct discussions with intellectuals and scholars in most of the countries we visited. We were given unprecedented access to people at the highest levels of government by whichever country was hosting us.

These were high-profile visits and we were treated as state guests. There were police cars, sometimes with sirens blaring, to escort us wherever we went. I did not care for this kind of travel, nor did many of the others on the commission. There was little chance to get a picture of these societies other than the one that the officials and bureaucrats wished to show us, or to see people who did not take the official line on political questions. It did not seem be in the spirit of the commission at all, but there was little the members could do about it.

It was also a source of dismay to many people when the office of the commission was set up in Geneva, rather than (say) Delhi or Nairobi or Bogotá or Dar es Salaam. But Nyerere decided that there was no other option. The commission had to conduct its business in an age before the internet, and the office had to be somewhere well connected to all the different countries represented by it. Even to this day, it is often not possible to travel from a country in Asia to a country in Africa without passing through Europe. Realism had to trump symbolism.

Despite the limits posed on our travels, there were memorable encounters. Our conversation with the president of Mozambique comes immediately to mind, where he described, without hyperbole or euphemism, the devastation wrought by the departing Portuguese at the moment of decolonization. When they left, he said, there was only one person in all of Mozambique who had completed high school. His description of the years of armed conflict in the country, of violent counter-revolutionaries who were willing to use child soldiers, will never leave me.

The most exciting of our visits was to Cuba. Fidel Castro's attitude to Nyerere bordered on reverence and we were all given royal treatment. We were invited to stay on the island for eight days and to travel everywhere, from beach resorts to hospitals and scientific laboratories. Castro frequently joined us on these visits. Even to my non-ideological eyes, there was much to admire in Cuba, in particular its achievements in providing access to inexpensive healthcare. At the end of our time there, Nyerere was sufficiently impressed by what he had seen to declare, 'We don't need a South Commission report. We don't need an alternative paradigm. It's here, Cuba's model!'

There was evident alarm in the room when he said this, particularly among such members as Shridath 'Sonny' Ramphal from Guyana and the commission's general secretary, Manmohan Singh (still a few years away from becoming India's most influential finance minister in recent years and even further away from his unexpected elevation to the office of prime minister in 2004). This tension between the more socialistic sympathies of Nyerere on the one hand and the more market-oriented sympathies of other members on the other meant—I am sorry to say—that over the course of three years, we lost the ethic and goal with which we started.

Few people were satisfied with the final document that emerged, the product of a complex series of negotiations between members and their outlook. I cannot say with a good conscience that the South Commission Report succeeded in its main aspiration, to be a document in which the countries of the south defined themselves and constructed a basis for economic reasoning grounded in our countries' experience. But perhaps this was only to be expected. The south was, and perhaps will always be, an idea in the making rather than something fully made. The lessons of the South Commission are to be found just as much in its history and the conversations it occasioned as in the report it eventually produced.

I have written in a different mode of these events, but these are personal memoirs, so I will not here try to give a detailed technical post-mortem or go into the politics and economics of the commission's deliberations. I would prefer to write here of something that happened after the commission's final meeting in Arusha, Tanzania, in October 1990. Once we came to the end of our official duties, Nyerere asked each of the members of the commission what we would like as a kind of 'gift'. Was there somewhere in Tanzania we would like to visit? Several members took up the opportunity for a safari in the Serengeti National Park. I asked him if I could meet his mother.

This wasn't a random request. Nyerere's mother had become, in a way, familiar to all the members of the commission because of how often he would refer to her in his conversations with us. She was a source of moral strength for him and a model of courage. He would go to her when he was struggling as president with the impact of the International Monetary Fund's demand that Tanzania, like other countries of the global south, make what were called 'structural adjustments' to its economy (liberalising trade, cutting subsidies, imposing fiscal discipline and so forth) as a condition for foreign aid. To his worries, she would say, 'Who is this IMF you're frightened of? You, who managed to fight the British Empire at the height of its power!' I was curious to meet my mentor's mentor.

I did indeed get to meet her, in their native village of Butiama in 1990. She was sitting on a wooden bedstead, quite like what in India is called a charpoy, with only a blanket worn as clothing. Nyerere told me he visited her often, if only so that he could scratch her back with a traditional back-scratching device, as she liked him to do. I was introduced to her as his shangazi, a Swahili word for a paternal aunt.

I stayed in Butiama for three unforgettable days. During the day, Mwalimu would take me to see the herd of cattle that he was rearing. Having observed the Amul dairy cooperative project in India where they processed milk from domestic cattle herds, whereas Africa depended on imports, he had decided to start a dairy farm in Tanzania. When he left the presidency, he had asked anyone who wished to give him a farewell present to gift him cattle.

In the evenings the extended family, who lived in a complex of homes, would sit in a circular hall-like space made of wood and bamboo. There were women with babies in their arms, children sitting on the floor, all watching and listening, and sharing their thoughts with him just as he shared his thoughts with them. He said he had more than a dozen mothers and had been brought up by all of them.

One conversation I had with him stuck in my mind. After one dinner, we had watched performances of various traditional local dances: lights, drums, spears, it was an incredible show. I was thrilled at the sight, and at the wonderful way in which these dances drew everyone in as participants, and told Nyerere this. He looked sober, almost hurt, then said, 'This is our tragedy—we dance and sing but do not get into the serious mode of labouring.' He meant, I think, that he wished that his people would bring a similar level of involvement and participation to economic and political activities, as he saw the Indians and Chinese doing. I simply accepted his judgement at the time. He would be so happy if he could see his Africa now, bubbling with energy and intellectual strength, and offering a front of solidarity to the others, with the African Union and many more such cross-continental groupings.

CHAPTER NINETEEN

A Dream Comes Home: Being in South Africa

While I was grieving over the failure of the South Commission to provide an economic take off for the former colonies, a gift landed in our laps. Lakshmi was invited by the President of India and his foreign minister to represent India in the newly liberated South Africa. Gopalkrishna Gandhi was the first high commissioner. He was recalled by President K.R. Narayanan to be his secretary. Narayanan and Inder Gujral, who was the prime minister, wanted to send someone who had been immersed in Gandhian philosophy and had experience of national reconstruction in post-Independence India. Lakshmi fitted that bill perfectly.

This was December 1997, and to our great good fortune, Nelson Mandela was still the president of the Republic of South Africa, though it was the last year of his presidency. South Africa's terrible experience of colonization and white domination had always evoked in us, not only anger at the cruelty of the regime and the regime itself, but also a deep desire to provide support.

India was the first country to raise its voice against apartheid and have the UN establish a special cell called the Anti-Apartheid Cell at the United Nations in New York. Then, there was Gandhi, a companion in our lives, who literally came to us from South Africa, where he had already experimented with his ideas of ashram life and satyagraha. The invitation to go to South Africa with a mission seemed like a gift that had been waiting for us at this time in our lives, when we had retired from our institutional work. Lakshmi was seventy-four and I was sixty-seven.

There was magic in our arrival in South Africa. We were received with a huge bunch of flowers, famous in South Africa—King Protea—and where did they come from? The wife of the vice-president, Zanele Mbeki, we were told. 'She is an admirer of yours, as she was present in Nairobi when you launched DAWN,' said the deputy high commissioner.

We had the good fortune of having friends in South Africa. I had met Graça Machel, who was known to be Mandela's partner and married him later that year, as a member of the Eminent Persons Group set up by the UN in 1996 to investigate as well as to make suggestions on the conditions of child soldiers in Liberia. She was a member of the group, as was Desmond Tutu.

South Africa at that time was a truly exciting place, full of what can be called, breaking out of the conventions. Women were an important presence in governance. The rigid hierarchies in official spaces that we know were not yet in place, so we could freely meet new people and learn about their work.

Memories of the apartheid years were still strong and we got to hear extraordinary stories of brutality and discrimination that seemed to belong to the Middle Ages, but also stories of courage and resistance. The Truth and Reconciliation Commission was the main subject of each day's news, and Lakshmi and I watched its proceedings every day with interest and anxiety.

Lakshmi's experiences in the cooperative movements, and mine in the international women's movement, gave us ways of relating to, and helping, our South African colleagues. In fact, it sometimes felt as if our whole life had been preparing us for our time in South Africa.

When Lakshmi and I went in for his swearing-in ceremony, after the formal moments, Nelson Mandela turned to me and said, 'Welcome, Mama, you are the only woman whom Graça knows in South Africa, she sends you greetings, you must come home.' And indeed Graça did reach out to me, took me with her to Mpumalanga where she was fostering a programme, engaging with the carers and families of HIV and AIDS patients.

We visited Soweto, and saw the Regina Munde Church where, during the apartheid regime, Archbishop Desmond Tutu had strengthened the black citizens and offered resistance to the white police—all famous incidents recorded in the narratives on the fight against apartheid in South Africa. We witnessed the stamping of feet, the toyi-toyi dance, as well as celebrations and the assertion of their rights by the black communities. Not surprisingly, given the colour consciousness of Indians, the officials in the high commission warned us against going to Soweto and advised that we should inform the government's security department and take security with us. Black areas were violent, they argued. Naturally, Lakshmi and I rejected this advice.

Other friends and freedom fighters, whether it was

members of the Sisulu family, South Africans of Indian origin such as Ahmed Kathrada and Ismail Meer as well as white supporters of the struggle such as Albie Sachs, an eminent lawyer, who was also incarcerated; the famous writer Nadine Gordimer, Helen Suzman a white woman who bravely supported Mandela and would be the 'postman' between his family and the prisoner (only white people were allowed to visit the prisoners on Robben Island), invited us home and shared their experiences and their analysis. Extraordinary men and women, such as Chief Justice Ismail Mohammad, and Frene Ginvala, the Speaker of the House, became close friends, sharing with us the history and the needs of the South Africa that was reborn. These friendships gave us access to so much knowledge. We heard in detail about the atrocities committed on the blacks, as well as about the various institutions and ideas put in place to divide South Africa.

Lakshmi's work in India of reviving and setting up institutions for the promotion and survival of handicrafts and handlooms, his participation in the refugee camps, post-Independence, his efforts and contribution to designing employment programmes while in the Planning Commission, for addressing agriculture—all came to bear fruit too. These became the resources that Lakshmi brought to the policy and programme councils and discussions in South Africa.

My experience with the women's movement, especially economic policy ideas, as well as building institutions, was welcomed by women whether in Parliament or fighting HIV and AIDS or setting up research centres. It was as if our lives had been arranged and filled just in order to channelize these experiences into the newly liberated South Africa. I spoke in the South African Parliament on the issue of whether the indigenous laws and cultural practices should be retained—arguing, of course, that they should be abandoned, as we know from Indian experience that traditional practices are punishing to women.

With support from the Ford Foundation, I arranged for a delegation of Indian and Pakistani women who had the experience of mobilizing women during elections to the legislatures, to brief the South African electoral commission and women's groups on engaging with the electoral education of women. There was such excitement when we called it an Indo-Pak delegation, as at that time India and Pakistan were deeply in conflict. The South African election commission hosted the delegation and took them around to several constituencies.

The strength of the bonds between the Mandelas and us was revealed by an invitation from them for their wedding which took place while we were there in 1998. I have a photo of the four of us, Madiba, Graça, Lakshmi and I, holding hands and dancing to a band that was playing at their wedding reception. We visited them before we left South Africa. I visited them again after we returned to India, and called on Mandela when he was bedridden.

Since I had met Desmond and Leah Tutu during the meetings of the Eminent Persons Group for studying the impact of war on child soldiers, especially in Liberia and Mozambique, I reached out to them and invited them to visit us in Pretoria. This began a friendship that was deep and wonderful.

Lakshmi, his brilliance clothed in gentleness, suggested simple ideas for dealing with the terrible curse of unemployment that South Africa was facing, which impressed the Tutus a great deal. They came to stay with us in Bangalore and even visited Lakshmi when he was in the ICU, fighting the final battle of his life. After Lakshmi died, they came to deliver the first Lakshmi Jain Memorial Lecture on November 5, 2013.

However, it was the deep friendship with Zanele Mbeki, at that time the wife of the vice-president of South Africa, that stayed and still continues my link with the Republic of South Africa. She would come to our home in Pretoria mid-morning, unannounced, just to talk! For hours we would sit in one of the smaller drawing rooms—she would relate the various beginnings of the resistance: how Julius Nyerere offered shelter in Tanzania to many of the people in resistance in South Africa, and enabled them to strengthen themselves.

South Africa had completed six years of 'freedom' from the apartheid regime, but already the cracks in the ethical standards of the leaders had begun to show. Freedom fighters, who had been appointed as ministers, were seeking more privileges and material attachments. This was disheartening for the likes of the Meers and the Kathradas: Ismail Meer, an eminent jurist who had defended Mandela in court, while Ahmed Kathrada had shared the prison cell with Mandela. Both were, as I have mentioned, South Africans of Indian origin who were deeply engaged with the anti-apartheid struggles.

Before we left the Republic, the Meers organized a meeting in Durban, a kind of farewell for us, and we were asked to speak and share with them our thoughts and ideas for the future of South Africa. We reminded them that this decay, namely the desire for loaves and fishes by the same persons who had been such brave self-sacrificing leaders during the struggle, had been the curse even in India. It seemed to be the experience in most countries, post-liberation. Human greed is a given and deprivation adds to the hunger. They felt soothed, as they were despondent that the dream of a just society, which had been their dream, was being corrupted by the very freedom fighters whom they considered noble.

My engagement with the Republic of South Africa and its women leaders continues even today and we partner on initiatives to strengthen their economic base as well as their voice. There is so much to share and exchange.

PART SEVEN

Requiem

'Om Bhur Bhuvah Swah, Tat Savitur Varenyam, Bhargo Devasya Dhimahi, Dhiyo Yo Nah Prachodayat.'

—Gayatri Mantra

CHAPTER TWENTY

Reflections on Loss

Akka

I am not sure my mind is ready for thoughts of mortality. But I can remember my mother's feelings about death. 'You are nothing once you are dead. You have barely stopped breathing and people are already packing up and thinking of the next task. Your body lies there, useless.'

Her nightmares, she told me, were of priests with white caste-marks on their foreheads, performing last rites. The thing to do, she said, was to live. She took good care of her health, moving away from antibiotics and other modern pills when she found they were making her weaker and coming to rely instead on herbal remedies. She sought all through her life to be self-reliant, and was ever vigilant about any loss of health.

In her last days, she was deeply frustrated by her own weakness. 'How did I get so seriously ill,' she asked. 'Just yesterday I was recovering. I feel helpless.' She hated being helpless, valuing her autonomy above all else. She tried her best not to sleep for fear that someone would administer some treatment she hadn't approved. She abhorred most of all the prospect of other people being in control of her posthumous existence, her reputation now in the hands of other people with their fallible, and biased, memories.

Even to her last, she was concerned most of all with the business of living: had the cows been brought in, did the cook know what her husband liked, were the children all right? She told me of the sari she planned to give me for my birthday, and of the sweets she had put aside for me in her room. I kissed her, overwhelmed by affection. And then the phlegm began to rise in her throat. The nurse rushed for a suction instrument to clear her breathing passages but it was too late by the time she returned. Where there had, even a few moments ago, been speech—worldly, engaged speech—there was an unworldly silence.

I recall what was said as her extended family contemplated her body—bearing out all her anticipations. One relative declared her a saint, soon to be reunited with the other departed souls. Someone else told us that we were not to cry, as our tears would be a burden on a spirit seeking liberation. Comparisons were made to Krishna and the Buddha. It was said repeatedly that she had died a good death, her family around her, and predeceasing her husband and so never to know widowhood.

The priest sprinkling holy water around the room to cleanse it of the pollution of death had tears in his eyes, as did the maids and the old gardener, all narrating their memories of her in her prime, and the many kindnesses she had done them, all recalling her fairness and generosity. She had not stopped looking alive, smiling and restful as she lay on the mat on the cold floor of the hall with the flame of an oil lamp flickering behind her head. Early dawn brought further colour to her face. This posthumous beatification was just what she had anticipated, and feared.

'I know what they'll do,' she had said. 'Put a portrait in the hall, garland, even worship it. But your place has already been taken by someone else.' She loathed those pictures. Her attitude to funeral rituals was one of abhorrence. She thought them humiliating—the stripping and washing of the body before an audience of onlookers, the placing of rice mixed with turmeric into the mouth of the dead person. The rituals symbolized the self slowly shedding the desires that mark the physical body. But my mother had no wish to be without those desires. To desire was to live, she thought, and the greatest desire was the desire for life. She could not take a view of death as a welcome exit.

She avoided those rituals if she could do so without giving offence, discouraged talk of them by family members and guests. Food from a feast after a funeral would be discreetly fed to the cattle. She wanted nothing morbid around her, nothing with the flavour of death to pollute her life.

Did she feel the mortification of being wrapped in white cloth, the colour she most disliked? Did she scream, I could not help wondering, when she was placed in the incinerator? I found it difficult to sleep, difficult to accept that she was gone, praying to the little statue of Krishna she had once given me that I might die in her stead, briefly believing that such a substitution was possible and that if I only wished it hard enough, she would come back.

I could not give up the desire to have her back, so on the night after her cremation I lay down in the same place in the hall where she had been laid down and prayed and prayed that I would be morphed into her and she would come back. I wished that my body would be replaced by her body. On another evening, I bought a basket of fragrant red roses and covered the image of Krishna with them and prayed that he would be moved to bring her back. In other words, I totally lost my mind.

For months, I let no one lay their hands on her saris, opening the wardrobe every now and then to take in their fragrance, her fragrance. I was only convinced to stop when my sister pointed out how badly my father took it when he saw the saris, and only then let her pack them away.

I gave up on these physical reminders. I tried instead to call to mind my memories of my mother at her most alive, our moments of intimacy. Such as the times when we would find ourselves alone in the house after my father had gone to play golf and the domestic chores were all done. She would ask me to sing, the drone of the tanpura I was strumming in the background, and listen with an intentness that showed more affection than any words, what my old tutor Iris Murdoch would have called 'loving attention'. It had a benign quality that I associate with the gaze of a loving god. Then my father would return, the sound of his footsteps on the stairs signalling his arrival. I would stop strumming and my mother would go to receive him: 'How was the game today?'

After his bath, they would go to their room and sit together awhile. He would make himself a glass of whisky soda, then make another, smaller, glass for her. 'Cheers,' she would say. It is her of whom I'm reminded by Shakespeare's remark about Cleopatra that custom could not stale her infinite variety.

Her death transformed my father's life—the large house in Bangalore was empty and he was occupying one bed in the room he had shared with my mother. My younger sister sensitively removed the second bed—the one that she used to lie on.

We had never imagined how much she had filled in that large building called Tharanga. It was this departure that showed us that it was a hollow house without her—no noise, no activity, just an elderly man living alone in a room in the house which had four bedrooms, two halls and large verandahs. It gave us some idea of how she had filled this big space with joy by constantly celebrating all of us—our birthdays, our children. It was unimaginable how that luminous active household transformed itself to emptiness. That reflection reveals what kind of light she was, something that perhaps we did not realize so well when she was alive.

Lakshmi

'He has started chest breathing,' the doctor said. 'He has three hours more.' He reported the fact casually, as if it were a cricket score. The 'he' was my beloved, Lakshmi. I shrieked for my sons, but they weren't within earshot. I rushed into his hospital room. His body was enmeshed in a nest of tubes, running into his neck, his wrist. His eyes were closed, his body tense. He was heaving, like someone carrying an impossibly weighty burden.

In 2009, Lakshmi had been diagnosed with a cancerous tumour in his intestines. We took him to Lilavati Hospital in Mumbai for treatment, where they performed a surgery. The surgery was successful, said the doctor, the lump had been removed and it looked like that was all there was. He recovered from the surgery pretty quickly and we were able to return home to Delhi and lead a normal life. We also had the benefit of blessings by the Dalai Lama, who gave me some pills, saying they were very precious but taken regularly they would protect him.

I was firm in my belief that not only would Lakshmi recover, he would not die before me. Long ago, Lakshmi had promised me that he would survive me, he would not let me get hurt or be ill-treated as it often happens when you are left behind. I took this statement by Lakshmi as seriously as all our other commitments. He was always like that in whatever he did—a person who kept his word, who knew my vulnerabilities and looked after me.

But there was a setback and there had to be a second procedure. Back we went to Lilavati Hospital, for another operation. He recovered, exactly as I thought he would. Then another surgery, from which he came out full of pep, so much so that the surgeons remarked on his stamina. But infections set in within the fortnight and he needed lung support in the ICU. He could not speak, except briefly and with a painful struggle to articulate the words. With a tube in his neck, he communicated mostly with his eyes, and sometimes, he would smile at me and make his mouth like a kiss.

When the nurses helped him to sit up in bed with his legs swinging over the side, he would look totally alert. One day, when I visited the room of the person in charge of the ICU and saw his chair, which was one of those cushioned chairs used by senior executives, I exclaimed: 'Oh, you should give this chair to Lakshmi, if you can sit him up in this he will soon be back on his feet.' I did not register at that time, the wry smile on that doctor's face, who perhaps knew that Lakshmi would not recover. He indulged me, I realized later, and said: 'Sure, I will send it across.'

Our sons and I thought that maybe his spirits would lift if he could move out of the ICU into a room. So we shifted him to a room and it looked as if that would revive him. He was aware of what was happening and actually thanked the various doctors and nurses who were there to see him out of the ICU. But once in the room, despite the entire support structure of the ICU having been brought up to the room, his strength declined.

At this stage, the doctors had nothing hopeful to tell us. When he began to heave and the doctor had made his grim pronouncement, there was nothing to do but to whisper in his ears, 'Lammu, it's over. The doctors say you have another three hours. Let us say the Jain mantra together.'

There was no intelligible response, just more heaving. I wondered where he was then. Was he thinking at all? Could he hear himself? Was he in pain? Was there anything I could do without disrupting the paraphernalia of tubes that divided him from me? I wanted to pick him up in my arms, comfort him, speak into his ear, kiss him. This distress lasted much longer than the doctor had forecast.

Three days later, we decided to take him by special aircraft to Delhi where he could be in his room and near his family. But the aircraft would not start. We were forced to return to the hospital, once again confined in the room, with my beloved alive but in pain.

We made another attempt—in the ambulance on the way to the aircraft, he tossed his head as if in a hysteria, and groaned intermittently. Once in Delhi, we tried repeatedly to induce him to open his eyes. But all he did was to groan, and put out his tongue, almost like clockwork. We inferred that it was a reflex, conditioned by his unconscious memory of the nurses asking him to put out his tongue in the ICU so that they could clean the saliva and mucous that would collect there while he was breathing through a lung pipe.

To this day I do not know how much of this he was aware of. But it was unbearable for us to watch, this tossing and groaning from a body marked in all its years by its quiet, controlled dignity. For three agonizing days this continued, until we asked the doctor to let him have some morphine. The groaning stopped, but it seemed that the only thing keeping him alive was the machine that kept his heart pumping, leaving us with the terrible question: was it time to withdraw life support?

After some hours of agonized deliberation, my sons and I asked for life support to be withdrawn. Even then, his heart continued to beat for nearly three hours. When I slipped my hand into his, he closed his hand over mine and gripped it. It shook me.

My lover, their father: so beautiful, so strong, so resilient. It was evident, painfully evident, that he had not wanted, had not been ready, to go. Even to this day I am tethered with the thought: 'Could he have lived?'

My mother had not wanted to go when she did. Nor had my husband. Why would one, when the life they had built around them was so pleasurable and full of love—that great unmatchable emotion.

Acknowledgements

I have said in these memoirs, that the desire to write about my experiences began when I was in my teens. But when I sat down to write this book, I found it an incredibly daunting task. Indeed, I requested a friend to write my biography for fear that if I wrote it myself, it would, like most people's memoirs, become a piece of self-promotion. However, Darren Walker of the Ford Foundation took the matter out of my hands by sending funds to the Ford office in Delhi, asking his colleagues to ensure that I wrote the book. It is a curious phenomenon how money drives the actions even of those who do not believe, or acknowledge, that money drives their actions. But the presence of these funds placed me under an obligation I could not ignore. My first thanks, then, are to Darren; I hope the following pages will justify his regard for me.

Darren's spontaneous action then received a big boost from the insistence by another dear friend, Gloria Steinem, that I write these memoirs. Gloria was, at that point, engaged in writing her own story from a sense of it needing to be told.

The project got going in earnest when my alma mater, St Anne's College, Oxford, offered me one of its Plumer Fellowships for a term. Professor Sally Shuttleworth, Senior Fellow at St Anne's, guided me to a number of relevant books and introduced me to Elleke Boehmer, Professor of English at Oxford, a novelist and the facilitator of the Oxford Centre for Life Writing, attached to Wolfson College, Oxford. I am grateful to St Anne's, its principal, Tim Gardam (2004–16), Fellows, administrative and catering staff, for reuniting me with Oxford, for nurturing me and giving me the nest I needed to start my introspective journey. In particular, I am grateful to the librarian, David Smith, and his assistants, for assembling a collection of biographies and autobiographies to guide me. A term as a visiting Fellow at Somerville College was another gift, again reading, listening and of course, the friendships. I am grateful to the former principal, Alice Prochaska, for her warmth and encouragement.

Elleke Boehmer generously offered to be my mentor as I wrote my memoirs. She and Professor Barbara Harris-White recommended me to Wolfson College for status as a visiting scholar. Elleke also recommended me to the English Faculty of the University of Oxford. I am grateful to the head of the faculty and to Sadie Slater, the finance officer, for their support, and to Alice Kelly for her research assistance in my early months of writing.

Wolfson provided me an environment of peace and natural beauty in which to think and write. I am grateful in particular to Rachael Connelly at the admission office, Rose Truby at the accommodation office, Louise Gordon, Phil Nixon, the IT officer, and Melanie Constantino, the gardener, each for the ways in which they enabled this memoir.

Since I was really lost on the 'how to' of constructing a memoir, I sought the help of many—three among them stand out for special mention. Indira Rajaraman, a brilliant public finance expert, and formerly my student, Pamela Phillipose, an equally brilliant writer and journalist, and Nikhil Pandhe, a doctoral student at Oxford when I first met him, but now a friend for all times.

I have always worked with others, many of them young women interested in research and in working with a feminist. I am grateful for the critical role played by Neha S Chaudhry, senior research assistant, who worked with me on the book for five years, in moving me along on my journey. I am also grateful for the assistance of Nakul Krishna in working with my drafts and giving my manuscript some shape.

I am beholden to Ravi Singh for accepting this story for publication and to Renuka Chatterjee for her skill as an editor, shaping the manuscript into a book!

This acknowledgement would not be complete without referring to my parents—Anna and Akka. Communication came naturally to them, a gift which they gave to their seven children. My life partner, Lakshmi Jain, was another source of inspiration and encouragement. Every day for several decades, he used to type away on an old Remington from 5 a.m., producing articles, memorandums and letters by the dozen. He wrote me a letter every day for eight years in longhand. I still have the pages which say 'I love you', in letters which go from small to big.

Losing him emptied me for a time of all energy and the will to live. So when Darren appeared with his encouragement to write, my sons Gopal and Vasu urged me to do it. They encouraged me and kept up a gentle pressure to ensure I completed what I had started, funding me, providing me with an office and assistance, commenting on my drafts and cheering me on as I wrote.